# Dorothy Macardle

## A Life

*Also published by The Woodfield Press*

*Trouble with the Law; Crimes and trials from Ireland's past*
LIAM CLARE & MÁIRE NÍ CHEARBHAILL (Eds)

*Dorothy Macardle: A life*
NADIA CLARE SMITH

*Print Culture and Intellectual Life in Ireland, 1660–1941: Essays in honour of Michael Adams*
MARTIN FANNING & RAYMOND GILLESPIE (Eds)

*Cesca's Diary 1913–1916: Where Art and Nationalism Meet*
HILARY PYLE

*The Gore-Booths of Lissadell*
DERMOT JAMES

*Differently Irish: a cultural history exploring twenty five years of Vietnamese-Irish Identity*
MARK MAGUIRE

*Documenting Irish Feminisms: The Second Wave*
LINDA CONNOLLY & TINA O'TOOLE

*Royal Roots – Republican Inheritance: The Survival of the Office of Arms*
SUSAN HOOD

*The Politics and Relationships of Kathleen Lynn*
MARIE MULHOLLAND

*St Anne's – The Story of a Guinness Estate*
JOAN USSHER SHARKEY

*Female Activists: Irish Women and Change 1900–1960*
MARY CULLEN & MARIA LUDDY (Eds)

*W & R Jacob: Celebrating 150 Years of Irish Biscuit Making*
SÉAMAS Ó MAITIÚ

*Faith or Fatherhood? Bishop Dunboyne's Dilemma*
CON COSTELLO

*Charles Dickens' Ireland: An Anthology*
JIM COOKE

*Red-Headed Rebel: A Biography of Susan Mitchell*
HILARY PYLE

*The Sligo-Leitrim World of Kate Cullen 1832–1913*
HILARY PYLE

*John Hamilton of Donegal 1800–1884*
DERMOT JAMES

*The Tellicherry Five: The Transportation of Michael Dwyer and the Wicklow Rebels*
KIERAN SHEEDY

*Ballyknockan: A Wicklow Stonecutters' Village*
SÉAMAS Ó MAITIÚ & BARRY O'REILLY

*The Wicklow World of Elizabeth Smith 1840–1850*
DERMOT JAMES & SÉAMAS Ó MAITIÚ
(Now back in print)

# Dorothy Macardle
## *A Life*

Nadia Clare Smith

THE WOODFIELD PRESS

This book was designed and typeset in 11pt on 14pt Sabon
by Carrigboy Typesetting Services for
THE WOODFIELD PRESS
17 Jamestown Square, Dublin 8
www.woodfield-press.com
e-mail: terri.mcdonnell@ireland.com

*Publishing Editor*
Helen Harnett

*Publisher*
Terri McDonnell

*House Editor*
Suzanna Henry

A catalogue record for this title is
available from the British Library

ISBN 978-1-905094-03-5

Printed in England
by Cromwell Press, Trowbridge

# Contents

# Acknowledgements

I AM INDEBTED TO MARIA LUDDY, who first suggested a biography of Dorothy Macardle at a conference in Liverpool in 2002, for her support for this project and for her scholarly generosity. Margaret Ó hÓgartaigh's friendship and intellectual support has been invaluable to me as well. I greatly appreciate the many insights about Irish women's history that Maria and Margaret have shared with me over the years in informal discussion as well as through their own scholarship. At Boston College, I would like to thank Rob Savage of the Irish Studies Program for his invaluable help and intellectual support over the years, and Kevin O'Neill and Peter Weiler of the History Department for their help and good counsel since I first began research on Irish women historians. I am indebted to Vera Kreilkamp, who kindly read and commented on a draft chapter on Dorothy Macardle's novels, and to Marjorie Howes for her help as well. Many thanks to other faculty members, friends, and students at Boston College who have helped with this book in various ways over the years, and to the staffs at the Burns Library and the O'Neill Library.

I would like to acknowledge the award of fellowships which provided some funding towards this project over the years, including a Fulbright Fellowship, awarded by the United States Fulbright Commission, and a Government of Ireland Post-Doctoral Research Fellowship, administered by the Irish Research Council for the Humanities and Social Sciences.

Many thanks to Terri McDonnell and her colleagues at The Woodfield Press for all their help with this book.

I would like to thank Peter Berresford Ellis for discussing Dorothy Macardle's life and work with me in the early stages of this project, and Ann Keating, Dorothy's god-daughter and friend, for sharing stories and personal knowledge about Dorothy. I am immensely grateful to Lelia Doolan for her generosity in sharing her vast knowledge of theatre with me, as well as her insights about Dorothy as a playwright. Many thanks to Gerardine Meaney and Luke Gibbons for discussing Dorothy's novels. I am indebted to Angus Mitchell for discussing my research with me, and for his scholarly generosity in sharing some of his own research on Irish historians and humanitarians in an international context. Thanks to Angela Bourke for pointing out connections between Dorothy Macardle and Maeve Brennan. Sinéad McCoole's work on Irish women in the revolutionary years was invaluable as I researched this phase of Dorothy's life. Eunan O'Halpin discussed *The Irish Republic* and Dorothy Macardle as a historian with me, and shared insights about Dorothy's life and friends in Dublin. Dónal Hall shared insights about Dorothy's Dundalk background. I would also like to thank participants at conferences in Ireland, Britain and the United States, who discussed my work with me at various stages. Thanks to Deirdre McMahon and others who commented on a paper on Dorothy Macardle which I presented at a Trinity College seminar, and to James Donnelly, Timothy Meagher, Gary Murphy and other participants at an American Conference of Irish Studies meeting in Milwaukee, when I presented a paper on Irish women historians in the Free State period. I am grateful to Mary O'Dowd and Ilaria Porciani, who organized a conference on European women historians in Galway in 2004, for discussing my work with me as well. Thanks also to Tom Desmond, Steve Quinn, and others at the National Library of Ireland, for all their help over the years. I would like to thank Cara, Maurice, and Laurence Wright for their friendship and support since I first began my research in Dublin. I am especially indebted to Maurice Wright for his early interest in this book, and for his much-appreciated encouragement.

I am grateful to the staffs at the National Library of Ireland, the National Archives of Ireland, the UCD Archives, the RTÉ Archives, Trinity College Library, Alexandra College Library, Mills College Library, the BBC Written Archives Centre, and the National Archives in Kew for helping to facilitate this project. Every reasonable attempt has been made to contact the copyright holders of material reproduced in this book.

# Introduction

THE TRAIN FROM DUBLIN TO BELFAST pulled up to the Dundalk station one October morning in 2000. When I looked out the window, I saw an old poster advertising the products of the Macardle brewery. I wished I could tear down the poster to keep as a souvenir, as I was familiar with one of the Macardles from my research on Irish women historians, but it might have meant getting stranded in Dundalk, and I was on my way to Belfast. When I returned to Dublin, I read some of Dorothy's letters, and she began to come to life. I located her house at 16 Herbert Place, where she lived when she began working on *The Irish Republic*, her magnum opus, in the 1920s. The area was popular with writers; her house was next to Elizabeth Bowen's birthplace, and one of Dorothy's flatmates was the novelist and historian Rosamond Jacob. Éamon de Valera often visited Herbert Place to discuss *The Irish Republic*. Dorothy also encountered uninvited guests there, including the occasional Irish Republican Army (IRA) man on the run, and, she was convinced, some disruptive poltergeists.

Many of Dorothy's personal papers, including journals and scrapbooks, were destroyed by her younger brother when she died in 1958, which meant that valuable evidence about her life was missing. Some of her letters, though, could be found in other collections. A biography would have to rely, in part, on less direct evidence, as well as on her published work and other people's observations. Her fiction contains emotional truths as well as autobiographical information, and her journalism provides insights into her thinking about politics, culture, and society. Her friend and one-time flatmate Rosamond Jacob kept an extraordinary diary, which made a reconstruction of Dorothy's life possible. As someone researching Dorothy's life, which featured more than a few mysteries as well as incomplete or missing evidence, and encountering occasional silences and evasions, I was able to relate to the psychic researchers and investigators who populate Dorothy's novels.

I also talked to people who had known Dorothy, and I was struck by occasional evasiveness when I asked about her mother, Minnie, who came from England. Was it simply the case that very little was known about her, or was she a Mrs Rochester, madwoman-in-the-attic[1] figure that no one wanted to talk about? Although Dorothy lived an Irish republican life, was there a slightly deranged English-woman at the center of it? I also encountered equivocation when I asked about Dorothy's personal life and romantic relationships. Was it true that she was "hopelessly in love with de Valera and could never look at another man," or was there anyone else?

Dorothy Macardle (1889–1958) was an important journalist and historian in twentieth-century Ireland, as well as a novelist, playwright, drama critic, political and social activist, and student of the occult. The international dimension of her life and work, as well as her versatility, makes her stand out from many of her counterparts. An Irish public intellectual with an international reputation, she narrated, from a republican perspective, the memory and meaning of the Irish revolution through her popular and influential political history, *The Irish Republic* (1937). Her monumental book, commissioned by Éamon de Valera, reached audiences on both sides of the Atlantic, and still occupies a significant, if ambiguous, place in Irish historiography. As a lifelong participant in both Irish and international political and intellectual exchanges, Dorothy's life story fits into multiple narratives and histories, including modern Irish political and social history, the history of women in interwar Europe, and the story of women historians and writers in the first half of the twentieth century.

Dorothy Macardle was a significant agent of political, social, and cultural change in twentieth-century Ireland. A republican activist in Ireland's War of Independence and Civil War, she supported her close friend Éamon de Valera and his Fianna Fáil party from the 1920s through the 1950s, sharing de Valera's goal of achieving a sovereign Irish republic through political means. Dorothy soon found that her secular, liberal vision of republicanism, which incorporated feminism

---

1   This phrase comes from Sandra M. Gilbert and Susan Gubar, *The Madwoman in the Attic: The Woman Writer and the Nineteenth-Century Literary Imagination* (New Haven and London: Yale University Press, 1979).

and internationalism, was often at odds with the official, more conservative nationalism promoted by church and state after Irish independence in 1922. She became a critical insider within Fianna Fáil while involving herself in campaigns for women's rights, civil liberties, and intellectual freedom. By the 1950s, she played a significant role within a circle of critical Irish intellectuals who contested the country's political, cultural, and intellectual climate, paving the way for the social changes of the 1960s and a more open, liberal, and less authoritarian society.

The career of Dorothy Macardle serves as an interesting and revealing case study concerning the course taken by politically active republican women after Irish independence in 1922. Historians have commented on the discrepancy between the active role played by republican women in achieving Irish independence, and their apparent silence and disengagement in independent Ireland. Dorothy's life and work present a different picture. As an engaged intellectual and feminist, she represented an alternative face of Irish womanhood that diverged from images promoted in mainstream discourse, and took on those images in her fiction.

Dorothy's political and social concerns can be situated and understood within an international context as well as an Irish one. Her political vision extended far beyond Ireland. She supported the goals of the League of Nations during the 1930s, when she interacted with humanitarian and feminist circles in Geneva who sought to promote social change through the League. After World War II, she transferred her support to the United Nations, the League's successor, and its humanitarian, cultural, and social sections. She acted on her humanitarian ideals by writing a second work of contemporary history, *Children of Europe* (1949), an account of the plight of children during and after the war, based on her own investigative journalism. An early and significant contribution to the social history of World War II and the Holocaust, her book functioned as an alternative to the standard military histories of the war. Overall, Dorothy's internationalism was a central component of her modern, liberal, cosmopolitan Irish identity.

As a historian and fiction writer, Dorothy contributed to key intellectual and literary debates from the 1920s to the 1950s. Her role as the author of *The Irish Republic* and *Children of Europe* locates her within the overlapping narratives of Irish historians and Western women historians in the first half of the twentieth century.

Her novels, situated in the literary world of the 1930s and 1940s, linked her with other writers of popular women's fiction of the period, and explored themes that still resonate today. Although only one of her novels was set in Ireland, all contain Irish and autobiographical dimensions. Dorothy's interest in the supernatural, which made its way into her novels and stories, demonstrated her engagement in a cultural debate that took place in England, where she lived for several years, as well as in Ireland.

Many of Dorothy's preoccupations continue to resonate a half-century after her death. The post-nationalist Ireland of the twenty-first century is a far more liberal and secular society than it was during her lifetime, and the status of women has been transformed. Her internationalist idealism still inspires many in Ireland who support the peacekeeping and humanitarian missions of the United Nations, as well as humanitarian non-governmental organizations such as Trócaire. *The Irish Republic* is still read, and historians and the Irish reading public continue to study and debate the Irish revolutionary period and the various interpretations of that period.

This book tells the story of an influential Irish woman historian and activist who operated in an Irish and international context. Dorothy's impact on Irish history and historiography was substantial. She was also a citizen of the world and a participant in events and debates taking place far from Ireland. Her life and work enhance and broaden our understanding of the political history of the newly independent Ireland, the history of women in Ireland and interwar Europe, Ireland in an international context, and Irish historiography. This book explores her many roles and identities, and places them in historical context.

Dorothy Macardle's distinctive liberal idealism motivated her actions, and her liberal ideals changed gradually in response to new circumstances. Her career challenges the notions that Irish women disengaged from political life in the Free State period, and that Irish republicans in the first half of the twentieth century were invariably insular, provincial, anti-modern, and disengaged from world events. She was a sophisticated, cosmopolitan figure whose engagement with global events and international currents of thought interacted with her Irish republican thinking. She deserves to have her multi-faceted story finally told.

CHAPTER ONE

# From Dundalk to Dublin, 1889–1916

T OY THEATRES, HAVING been popular for about a hundred years, were somewhat on the wane by the end of the nineteenth century. However, for Dorothy Macardle, a girl growing up in Ireland in the 1890s, her toy theatre, with its "sets of scenery and cardboard figures, the complete stuff of some half-dozen gorgeous plays," provided "such a sense of riches and mastership,"[1] and foreshadowed her career as a playwright, in addition to offering an imaginative escape from domestic dramas enacted in her well-appointed Dundalk home.

Dorothy Margaret Callan Macardle was born in Dundalk, County Louth on 7 March 1889.[2] Her parents, Thomas Callan Macardle and Minnie Lucy Ross Macardle, eventually had four more children; Kenneth (nicknamed Dick) was born in 1890, John in 1892, Gladys Monica (called Mona) in 1894, and Donald in 1900. The staff members of the prosperous Macardle household at 5 Seatown Place included Honora Aughney, the governess, Annie Rice, the housemaid, Sarah Fearon, the nurse, and Catherine Sands, the cook.[3] The

1 Dorothy Macardle, *The Uninvited* (New York: Literary Guild of America, 1942), 65. She still cherished her toy theatre as an adult. Rosamond Jacob Diary [hereafter RJD], National Library of Ireland [hereafter NLI], MS 32,582 (51), 6 April 1926. In Dorothy's novel, *The Uninvited*, her protagonist, Roderick Fitzgerald, describes a toy theatre his godmother had given him. See also Antonia Fraser, *A History of Toys* (Delacorte Press, 1966), 128–40.
2 Birth Certificate of Dorothy Macardle, General Register Office, Dublin.
3 Census of Ireland, 1901, Louth, 41 D.E.D. Dundalk Urban no. 4, 35.

Macardles were comfortably located within the upper strata of the middle classes. Most middle-class households in Britain at the turn of the century were only able to employ one servant, rather than a staff.[4]

Thomas Callan Macardle, born in Dundalk in 1856, came from a prominent Irish Catholic family whose fortunes were linked with Dundalk's history as a brewing centre. His father, Edward Henry Macardle, had established a brewery in 1862 with his business partner, A.T. Moore, and Macardle Moore became one of Ireland's leading breweries.[5] Edward Macardle married Margaret Callan of Tullagee, County Louth, in the early 1850s. The couple had nine children, including one son who became a Jesuit.[6] Thomas Macardle attended St Mary's College in Dundalk, and later lived in England with the family of his cousin, steamship owner John Williams.[7] Edward Macardle died in 1887, leaving a considerable fortune of over six thousand pounds. His widow, Margaret, remained in her substantial home in the Cambricville area of Dundalk, where she lived with several of her unmarried children until her death in 1921.[8]

Thomas returned to Dundalk to run the Macardle Moore brewery shortly after his father's death, and his careers in business and politics flourished between the 1890s and the early 1920s. He became the chairman of other enterprises besides the brewery, and served as a Justice of the Peace and as President of the Dundalk Chamber of Commerce.[9] In Dundalk, "the military and commercial interests enjoyed a warm working relationship," and Macardle Moore benefited financially from the Union between Ireland and Britain, and from Dundalk's position as a garrison town. The brewery supplied

---

4 Carol Dyhouse, *Feminism and the Family in England, 1880–1939* (Oxford: Basil Blackwell, 1989), 109.
5 *Tempest's Annual* (Jubilee Annual 1909), 107; Harold O'Sullivan, *Dundalk and North Louth: Cúchulainn's Country* (Donaghadee, N. Ireland: Cottage Publications, 1997), 42.
6 See "The Old Callan Family of Dromiskin," *Dundalk Democrat*, 1 March 1930; Dundalk and Kane Parish Register, 1850–72; Will of Margaret Macardle, P.R. Will Dundalk, D.O.G. 14 March 1922, National Archives of Ireland, Dublin [hereafter NAI]; *Tempest's Annual* (Jubilee Annual 1909), 97.
7 1881 (England) Census, Civil Parish Poulton Cum Seacombe, Registration District Birkenhead.
8 Will of Edward Henry Macardle, [89] Armagh, D.O.G. 24 May 1887. NAI, Census of Ireland, 1901 Louth, 40/D.E.D. Dundalk Urban no. 3, 4.
9 Macardle, Sir Thomas Callan, K.B.E., *Who Was Who, 1916–28*, 657; *Thom's Directory* (Dublin, 1921). Other concerns he headed were the Dundalk and Newry Steampacket Co., the Dundalk Race Co., Kinahan Bros., and Alpha Trust.

beer to the British army regiments stationed in Dundalk and in the Curragh in Kildare, and Macardle Moore later became known as "The Irish Army Brewers."[10]

Thomas married an Englishwoman, Minnie Lucy Ross, in a Catholic ceremony in Dublin on 24 April 1888. Minnie, who came from an Anglican family, appears to have converted to Catholicism when she married.[11] Minnie Lucy Hicks, later Ross, was born in Norwood, Surrey, in 1860, the daughter of Isabella and James Clarke Hicks.[12] In 1857, sixteen-year-old Isabella Lucy Ross of Matlock Bath, Derbyshire, and twenty-one-year-old James Hicks, son of Dr Robert Hicks of Baslow, Derbyshire, were married at the Anglican church in neighboring Matlock.[13] James changed his surname to Ross in 1864, and his children's names were changed to Ross as well. It was later thought that James was the eldest son of James Clark Ross, the celebrated nineteenth-century polar explorer.[14] James Clarke Ross served as a cornet in the 18th Dragoons before becoming a paymaster and an honorary captain in the Scots Greys. In 1879, he became a staff paymaster in the Army Pay Department with the honorary rank of major, and later with the honorary rank of Lieutenant Colonel. The Rosses moved frequently with the regiment prior to James' appointment to the Army Pay Department. Minnie's younger sister Mary was born in Ireland, and her sister Isabel in Scotland.[15]

Minnie retained her English cultural identity and fervent support for British imperialism, which in turn influenced her children's identity formation. The daughter of a British soldier and the niece of Col. William Hicks, killed in action in the Sudan in 1883, Minnie was "herself a little soldier, every fragile inch of her." Thomas, a

---

10 Donal Hall, *World War I and Nationalist Politics in County Louth, 1914–1920* (Dublin: Four Courts Press, 2005), 30–1.

11 Marriage Certificate of Thomas Macardle and Minnie Lucy Ross, General Register Office [hereafter GRO], Dublin. Minnie, whose parents were Anglican, was listed as a Roman Catholic in the 1901 Census.

12 Birth Certificate of Minnie Lucy Hicks, General Register Office of England.

13 Marriage Certificate of James Clarke Hicks and Isabella Lucy Ross, General Register Office of England.

14 Peter Tremayne, "A Reflection of Ghosts," in Stephen Jones and Jo Fletcher, eds., *Gaslight and Ghosts* (London: Robinson, 1988), 87. Maurice J. Ross, in *Polar Pioneers: John Ross and James Clark Ross* (Montreal, 1994), wrote that James Clark Ross' eldest son was named James Coulman Ross. Ross, 285.

15 I am indebted to Edith Philip of the National War Museum of Scotland for information about James Clarke Ross. Edith Philip to author, 4 February 2005. For the Ross family, see also the Census of England, 1881, and the Census of Scotland, 1891.

moderate Irish nationalist who supported Home Rule, generally
tolerated his wife's views, but political differences in the Macardle
household sometimes led to tension, particularly when Thomas came
home one day to find the front hall bedecked with Union Jack
pennants. Minnie decorated the children's nursery with pictures of
Queen Victoria and British military heroes, glorified the British Army
and the Empire, and took Dorothy to see the royal procession when
Queen Victoria visited Dublin in 1897. Dorothy enthusiastically
embraced her mother's political allegiances and veneration of Queen
Victoria as a child, and did not develop a sense of Irish identity until
she was older.[16]

Minnie Macardle remains a somewhat mysterious figure long after
her death. She appears to have felt isolated and depressed in Dundalk,
separated from her family in England. Evidence suggests that Dorothy
felt her mother was inadequate, and that Minnie may have been
moody and volatile. Absorbed in her own unhappiness, she may have
been incapable of being the loving, understanding, supportive mother
that Dorothy wished for, and the relationship between the two was not
close.[17] Dorothy may also have noticed tensions between Minnie and
Thomas and his family. Her novels feature several unhappy couples,
and one depicts a particularly acrimonious relationship between a
woman and her mother-in-law, perhaps partly based on Minnie's
relationship with Margaret Macardle.[18] Dorothy's relationship with
Minnie helped shape not only her personality and relationships, but her
politics and fiction as well. As she searched for alternative relationships
and families and communities as a young adult, she found them in
unexpected places, including a women's college in Dublin and the
community of Irish nationalists.

Like other privileged children in Britain and Ireland at the time,
Dorothy and her younger siblings spent their earliest years being
looked after by a nurse. During the day, they played in an upstairs
nursery, where they also had their meals. The nurseries of wealthy

16  Dorothy Macardle, Bureau of Military History, 1913–21, Statement by Witness,
    National Archives of Ireland [hereafter NAI] BMH/457; Dorothy Macardle,
    "The Young Victorian," Broadcast Talk, RTÉ Written Archives, 25 August 1956.
17  After hearing Dorothy talk about her mother, her friends came to view Minnie in
    highly negative terms and dislike her. Ann Keating [daughter of Dorothy's friend
    Linda Kearns MacWhinney], letter to author, 14 June 2004. See also RJD, NLI
    MS 32,582 (45), 30 June 1924; RJD NLI MS 32,582 (55), 15 December 1926;
    RJD NLI MS 32,582 (62), 5 August 1929.
18  Dorothy Macardle, *The Seed Was Kind* (London: Peter Davies, 1944).

children at the turn of the century were filled with toys such as rocking horses, toy soldiers, elaborate dollhouses, and sumptuously dressed dolls, and upper-class girls might be just as lavishly dressed as their dolls. In the 1890s, Dorothy, a girl with long brown hair and large, wide-set, serious blue eyes, would probably have worn short dresses with puffed sleeves and sashes, black stockings, and laced boots, and her hair would have been plaited or tied back with ribbons. Dorothy's walks around Dundalk with her nurse and siblings were less than pleasurable. She disliked the dirt and noise of the town and was deeply disturbed when she encountered destitute children. She wished she lived in "beautiful England" rather than Dundalk. Following their walks, the children were served afternoon tea in the nursery, with the housemaid bringing up trays of bread and butter and scones. At night, they retired to the night nursery, where the nurse also slept.[19]

As a child, Dorothy's imagination was captured by books, and she developed a lifelong interest in literature as well as in drama. Like other late-Victorian children, she read lavishly illustrated volumes of fairy tales by Hans Christian Andersen, the Grimms, and Charles Perrault, as well as *The Arabian Nights*, which she found "dazzling in its originality, so abounding in color, movement, invention, and fantasy."[20] British and Irish girls read about the adventures of boarding-school girls in the school stories that became popular in the 1880s, as well as classic nineteenth-century novels such as *Jane Eyre* and *Little Women*.[21] The 1890s and early 1900s were a transitional time in children's literature, in which images of independent, adventurous girls coexisted with older images of meek, well-behaved girls from the nineteenth century. While Dorothy enjoyed reading classic fairy tales as a child, one of her favourite books was Lewis

---

19  Macardle, "The Young Victorian." See Enid Starkie, *A Lady's Child* (London: Faber and Faber, 1941), 28–34, 72, which describes the domestic world of an upper-class Dublin child in the early twentieth century. Photographs from the 1890s show young girls dressed in the way described. See, for example, photographs of Dorothy's exact contemporary and fellow historian, Eileen Power, as a child in England in the 1890s, in Maxine Berg, *A Woman in History: Eileen Power, 1889–1940* (Cambridge: Cambridge University Press, 1996), 16, 19. Novelist Elizabeth Bowen described walks with her governess in early-twentieth-century Dublin. See Bowen, *Seven Winters: Memories of a Dublin Childhood* (New York: Alfred A. Knopf, 1962), 15–27.

20  Dorothy Macardle, "Pass-word to Fairy Land," *Irish Press*, 14 December 1932, 6; Macardle, "The Young Victorian."

21  Sally Mitchell, *The New Girl: Girls' Culture in England, 1880–1915* (New York: Columbia University Press, 1995), 74–5, 143.

Carroll's *Alice's Adventures in Wonderland*, which gave her "something that all children long for – a sense of power."[22] She liked how the book featured an intelligent girl who "likes using her brains," and, more subversively, "tell[s] kings and queens to their faces that nobody cares for them."[23] Dorothy, an intellectually gifted, spirited young girl, clearly appreciated intelligent, active young heroines in fiction, rather than the passive, self-effacing girls who populated morally earnest works of Victorian children's literature. Moreover, she may have wished that she too could tell adults, such as her mother, that she disliked them.

A turn-of-the-century survey revealed that a great many girls in the British Isles wanted to be famous authors when they grew up,[24] and Dorothy might have been one of them. Her earliest efforts as a writer may have begun in childhood or early adolescence. "The themes and codes and cues of many women's fantasy life become set between eleven and fourteen," a literary scholar proposes, and "a continuous thread connects the daydreams of some girls who grew up to become authors [and] the fictions they wrote (as adults)."[25] In Dorothy's case, this may have involved the filtering and transmission of childhood daydreams about breaking free of her mother and having a different family into novels in which the young heroines repeatedly confront and break free of oppressive mother figures, and successfully move on to maturity and marriage and new families. As her novels "enact situations that must be compulsively repeated,"[26] they may provide emotional truths and important insights about Dorothy's emotions and daydreams as a girl and as an adult.

The Macardle children's early social lives included occasional parties, trips to the theatre, and holidays in Ireland and abroad. Children's parties in affluent British and Irish society might feature magicians, Punch-and-Judy shows, large quantities of iced cakes, and music and dancing for older children.[27] As an adult, Dorothy enjoyed giving parties, but by then her guests played charades and told ghost stories. The Macardle siblings, like other Irish and English children,

---

22  Dorothy Macardle, "Magic and Logic, the Immortality of Alice," *Irish Press*, 26 May 1932, 7.
23  Macardle, "Magic and Logic," 7.
24  Mitchell, *The New Girl*, 147.
25  Mitchell, *The New Girl*, 143–4.
26  Mitchell, *The New Girl*, 147.
27  Starkie, 136–7.

would have been taken to traditional pantomimes at Christmas, and occasionally to plays where even small children were part of the audience, such as productions of Shakespeare's works.[28] As a young theatre enthusiast, Dorothy may have put on plays with her siblings, as Mona and Donald were also interested in the stage, in addition to playing with her beloved toy theatre.

Holidays also featured in the lives of affluent late-Victorian children in Ireland and Britain. While trips to local seaside resorts were especially popular with affluent Irish families,[29] the Macardles were also able to travel abroad, and Dorothy visited France, Belgium, and Switzerland as a child, as well as England where her maternal relatives lived.[30] She remained an inveterate international traveller throughout her life. However, as she and her mother both suffered from indifferent health, some of their travel to England and the Continent may have involved seeking treatments and going to spas and sanatoria.[31] Dorothy experienced occasional severe headaches and underwent several operations on her head during her life, and developed lung problems which worsened in later years.[32] One of her novels, *Uneasy Freehold*, features a fragile and vulnerable young woman who experiences a sense of helpless rage about her condition and fears incarceration, either at home or in an institution. The emotionally unstable Stella is sedated by a doctor and forcibly confined to her bedroom by her morbid, forbidding grandfather, who threatens to send her to a nursing home run by the mad Miss Holloway, and Stella subsequently acts out by destroying things.[33] Dorothy's temperament was rebellious rather than passive and quiescent, and as a girl who craved freedom and independence, she must have felt intensely frustrated by the illnesses which kept her confined to bed for long periods.

28 Starkie, 102–3
29 Alan Hayes, ed., *The Years Flew By: Recollections of Madame Sidney Gifford Czira* (Galway: Arlen House, 2000), 11.
30 Dorothy Macardle, "How Bridges Beautify Cities," *Irish Press*, 13 January 1932, 6. In this article, Dorothy referred to a childhood visit to Bruges, Belgium. Rosamond Jacob referred to Dorothy discussing stays in Switzerland and the Isle of Wight. RJD, NLI MS 32,582 (49), 7 August 1925.
31 In England, Dorothy once accompanied her mother to Bath to seek treatment. RJD, NLI MS 32,582 (61), 5 July 1929. See also Dorothy Macardle to Owen Sheehy Skeffington, Sheehy Skeffington Papers, NLI MS 40,505 (5), 8 December 1937.
32 RJD, NLI MS 32,582 (49), 10 August 1925.
33 Dorothy Macardle, *Uneasy Freehold* (London: Peter Davies, 1941), 244–5.

Many upper-class British and Irish children at the turn of the
century were not especially close to their parents, with whom they
spent little time.[34] Like her peers, Dorothy was attended to by nurses
and governesses, and may have only seen her parents for a short
period each day. In these households, there was a clear demarcation
between the upstairs world of the nursery and the downstairs world
of adults, and parents "seemed to belong to another world, a world
separated from [children] by a great, insurmountable China wall."[35]
She may have suspected, though, that all was not right with her family.

Dorothy's parents, whose relationship seems to have become
increasingly strained during her adolescence, were living apart by the
time she was a young adult. Minnie moved to London, while Thomas
remained in Dundalk.[36] In Dorothy's novels, two marriages of incompatible couples end in separation. Suzette, in *Fantastic Summer*, leaves
her husband and son in Ireland and settles in France, where she soon
dies, but her memory haunts the other characters after her death.
Lydia, in *Dark Enchantment*, divorces her husband and ultimately
abandons her daughter by escaping to South America. Uncongenial
English wives and mothers feature prominently in Dorothy's novels,
and her fictional heroines cope with feelings of abandonment by their
mothers, as well as resentment towards them. Suzette and Sybil, in
*The Seed Was Kind*, who in different ways resemble the unfortunate
Minnie, are blamed most vehemently by other characters for the
failure of their marriages, and their respective husbands are presented
as suffering intolerably from their wives' difficult personalities.[37]
Dorothy, then, may have viewed her father, with whom she had a
good relationship, as a long-suffering victim of her mother.

As Dorothy grew older, she came into increasing conflict with her
mother. This was not uncommon in late Victorian and Edwardian
families in which the daughter was serious and intellectually ambitious,

---

34  Carol Dyhouse, *Girls Growing Up in Late Victorian and Edwardian England*
(London: Routledge and Kegan Paul, 1981), 23.
35  Starkie, 36.
36  Census of Ireland, 1901, Louth, 41 D.E.D. Dundalk Urban no. 4, 35; Census of
Ireland, 1911, Louth, 41 D.E.D. Dundalk Urban no. 3, 1. The family lived
together in Dundalk in 1901, but only Thomas lived in Dundalk in 1911. Minnie
lived in London for the rest of her life.
37  Dorothy Macardle, *Uneasy Freehold* (London: Peter Davies, 1941); Macardle,
*The Seed Was Kind* (London: Peter Davies, 1944); Macardle, *Fantastic Summer*
(London: Peter Davies, 1946); Macardle, *Dark Enchantment* (London: Peter
Davies, 1953).

1. Dorothy Macardle, 1919. (Courtesy of Alexandra College Dublin)

and the socially conventional mother was unable to understand or support her daughter's goals.[38] A young girl craving independence and intellectual engagement might actively resent her mother as a particularly negative authority figure who demeaned her or obstructed her goals by insisting on conformity. The girl's relationship with her father might be far less tense.[39] Dorothy staged an intense mother-daughter drama in her most personal novel, *The Seed Was Kind*. Diony and her mother, Sybil, have an acrimonious relationship because Diony is serious and earnest, while Sybil is superficial, selfish, and unsympathetic to her daughter's goals and ideals. Despite the tensions in their relationship, Dorothy kept in touch with her mother, who needed an attendant during the last decades of her life due to her

38  Macardle, "The Young Victorian;" Macardle, "The Dublin Student," Broadcast Talk, RTÉ Written Archives, 1 September 1956. See also Dyhouse, *Girls Growing Up in Late Victorian and Edwardian England*, 16, 32.
39  See, for example, Starkie, 231, 273–7, for her conflicts with her mother during her adolescence; Dyhouse, *Feminism and the Family in England*, 11; Elizabeth Grubgeld, *Anglo-Irish Autobiography: Class Gender, and the Forms of Narrative* (Syracuse: Syracuse University Press, 2004), 77–89.

severe rheumatoid arthritis, and occasionally visited her in London.
She talked with friends about her mother and their relationship, and
one friend, who considered Dorothy "unfortunate" to have such a
"beast" for a mother, wondered how the Macardle siblings could be
so attentive to Minnie.[40]

Overall, Dorothy's family and upbringing influenced her in several
ways. The Macardle family's wealth and social position gave her
social and educational resources that helped her negotiate adulthood
and independence. Dorothy was highly conscious of social class, and
gained a sense of privilege and social confidence from her background.[41] Her family also shaped her views on marriage and mother-
daughter relations, and her experience with difficult family relationships
may have contributed to an avoidance of emotional intimacy in adult
relationships.[42] Her feelings about her family made their way into
fictional works combining emotional truths and disguised autobiographical subtexts.

Dorothy was educated at home by a governess, Honora Aughney,
until her teens.[43] Her education followed a familiar pattern for upper-
middle-class girls in the British Isles at the time, many of whom never
attended school, or spent only a few years at exclusive private schools
during their adolescence. When they had outgrown the nursery, they
would spend their days in the schoolroom with the governess. As
Dorothy and her younger brothers Kenneth and John were close in
age, they shared instruction with Miss Aughney in the schoolroom
before going to boarding schools. Kenneth and John were eventually
sent to the Oratory School, an elite Catholic institution in Edgbaston,
England.[44] Dorothy resented the restrictions she faced as a girl, and
envied her brothers their educational opportunities and escape from
Dundalk. As a young adolescent she became depressed and anxious
about her future. She felt isolated and restrained in Dundalk, and

---

40 RJD, NLI MS 32,582 (55), 15 December 1926; RJD, NLI MS 32,582 (45), 30
June 1924; Ann Keating to author, 14 June 2004; Minnie Lucy Macardle, Death
Certificate, General Register Office, Southport.
41 For her reflections on social class, see *Alexandra College Dublin Magazine*, vol.
11 (June 1952), 6–9.
42 A friend felt, for example, that Dorothy's dislike of emotional intimacy helped
lead to the termination of a close friendship. See RJD, NLI MS 32,582 (72), 31
March 1933.
43 NAI, Census of Ireland, 1901, Louth, 41 D.E.D., Dundalk Urban No. 4, 35.
44 War Office 339/28290, National Archives, Kew. For a discussion of schoolrooms
and governesses in upper-middle-class households, see Dyhouse, *Girls Growing Up
in Late Victorian and Edwardian England*, 40–6.

longed for freedom and independence and intellectual fulfillment. Her crisis lasted until she escaped to school in Dublin. Dorothy later came to see this period as crucial in her social and political development, as it made her feel rebellious and reinforced her longing for freedom and opposition to injustice.[45]

Although Dorothy later became intensely interested in Irish and international politics, her early upbringing and education sheltered her from knowledge about political developments in Ireland and the wider world.[46] Dundalk, a provincial port city north of Dublin, was located at some distance from the political and cultural developments then animating the capital. Dorothy's mother was a Unionist, and her father was a moderate nationalist who favoured Home Rule, rather than a republican advocating Irish independence.[47] In later years, Dorothy developed views on Irish nationalism that were greatly at variance with those held by her family.[48] Other Irish girls with similar backgrounds shared this experience of being insulated from an understanding of Irish nationalism. Enid Starkie grew up in a wealthy Catholic Unionist home in Dublin in the Edwardian era with parents who were hostile to nationalism, and Sidney Gifford, who grew up in Dublin in an affluent, religiously mixed Unionist household, was not allowed to read nationalist literature at home. In contrast, another contemporary of Dorothy's, Rosamond Jacob, who came from a middle-class Quaker nationalist family in Waterford, developed a political consciousness as a child and followed Irish nationalist politics as well as international events at the turn of the century.[49]

Dorothy and others of her generation were living through a highly significant period in Irish history. During her childhood and adolescence, political and cultural developments were taking place that would transform Ireland. Throughout the nineteenth century, Irish nationalists had contested the Act of Union with Britain using both political and violent methods. Elsewhere in the world, other nationalist movements were emerging to challenge the British Empire.

45 Macardle, "The Dublin Student."
46 Dorothy Macardle, *Alexandra College Dublin Magazine*, vol. 11 (June 1952), 6–9.
47 Donal Hall, *World War I and Nationalist Politics in County Louth, 1914–1920* (Dublin: Four Courts Press, 2005), 7–12, 30–3.
48 Dorothy Macardle, Statement by Witness, NAI BMH/457.
49 Starkie, *A Lady's Child*; Alan Hayes, ed., *The Years Flew By: The Recollections of Madame Sidney Gifford Czira* (Galway: Arlen House, 2000), 11; RJD, NLI MS 32,582 (2), 10 April 1900.

In the 1880s, the charismatic Charles Stewart Parnell led the Irish
Parliamentary Party, which promoted Home Rule, or limited autonomy for Ireland within the British Empire. Home Rule bills were
defeated in Parliament in 1886 and 1893, but the Irish Party maintained its popularity in Ireland and continued to promote Home Rule
under Parnell's successor, John Redmond. International events,
particularly the Boer War between Britain and the Boer republics in
South Africa, reverberated in Ireland, with many Irish nationalists
supporting the Boers. Dorothy, in contrast, was a pro-British "jingo"
during the Boer War of 1899–1902, singing "Soldiers of the Queen"
incessantly with her younger brothers. Irish cultural nationalism,
which would later exert a strong influence on Dorothy and reshape
her political thinking, flourished between 1890 and 1914. Cultural
developments with political ramifications included the founding of
the Gaelic League, with its mission to revive the Irish language, in
1893, and the Irish Literary Theatre, the precursor of the Abbey
Theatre, in 1899. Sinn Féin, an advanced nationalist movement that
represented an alternative to both the Irish Party and militant secret
societies such as the Irish Republican Brotherhood, was founded by
Arthur Griffith in 1905. Sinn Féin branches were soon established
throughout Ireland, and a Dundalk branch was founded in 1907 and
led by Patrick Hughes. Sinn Féin advocated a program of Irish self-
sufficiency and non-cooperation with Britain, culminating in its
boycott of the British Parliament following the 1918 elections, when
successful Sinn Féin party candidates established an alternative
Parliament called Dáil Éireann in Dublin.[50]

Dorothy left Dundalk for Dublin when she was sixteen to continue
her education at Alexandra College.[51] In Dublin, she lived first at 101
Lower Baggot Street, and later at 1 Wellington Road, before moving
to 5 Earlsfort Terrace in 1911.[52] Alexandra College, founded in 1866
by Anne Jellicoe, was one of the leading educational establishments
for young women in Ireland. As the college and its lower division,

50 See Patrick Maume, *The Long Gestation: Irish Nationalist Life 1891–1918* (New
   York: St Martin's Press, 1999); P.J. Mathews, *Revival: The Abbey Theatre, Sinn
   Féin, the Gaelic League, and the Co-operative Movement* (Cork: Cork University
   Press, 2003); Macardle, "The Young Victorian"; Hall, *World War I and Nationalist
   Politics in County Louth*, 12–13.
51 Macardle, "The Dublin Student."
52 *Alexandra College Dublin Magazine* [hereafter *ACD Magazine*], vol. 4, no. 30
   (June 1907), 58.

Alexandra School, were under Church of Ireland management, students were often drawn from wealthy and middle-class Protestant and Unionist families, and Dorothy was one of the few Catholics in attendance. Alexandra College initially offered university-level instruction, which enabled the students to take the Royal University of Ireland's degree examinations and earn a B.A. Trinity College, which like Alexandra had a predominantly Protestant and Unionist student body, opened its degrees to women in 1904, while the constituent colleges of the National University of Ireland, located in Dublin, Cork and Galway, followed in 1908. Once women were admitted to the two universities in Dublin, university courses at Alexandra were phased out.[53] Dorothy arrived at Alexandra during a transitional period and attended lectures both at Alexandra and at the new University College Dublin as she worked towards her B.A. degree.[54]

Dublin opened up a new world to an intellectually inclined young woman like Dorothy, with her love of literature and the theatre, providing a sense of freedom she had never enjoyed at home. Alexandra was located on Earlsfort Terrace, near University College Dublin and St Stephen's Green and the centre of Dublin. The college was a stately redbrick Victorian building, and its grounds featured a goldfish pond and flower gardens where Dorothy and her friends could "sit under the trees and either study or talk, talk, talk."[55] While Alexandra students could enjoy a cherished sense of freedom and full social lives, they were also part of an intellectual, all-female community where their academic ambitions and career goals were taken seriously. Dorothy experienced a welcome sense of community at Alexandra, which she considered "an earthy Paradise," and met stimulating teachers and role models such as Miss Webb, a gifted lecturer in English literature, Miss Shillington, who lectured in French, and Miss White, the principal, who enjoyed discussing poetry with students.[56] She encountered women who modeled social engagement through the

---

53  Anne V. O'Connor and Susan Parkes, *Gladly Learn and Gladly Teach: Alexandra School and College, 1866–1966* (Dublin: Blackwater Press, 1984). The Royal University of Ireland became the National University of Ireland in 1908, and from then on, the predominantly Catholic and nationalist NUI students, both male and female, could earn degrees by attending one of three constituent university colleges.

54  *Alexandra College Dublin Magazine*, vol. 5 (December 1912), 40.

55  Mary Manning, "The Schoolgirls of Alexandra," *Irish Times*, 3 June 1978.

56  O'Connor and Parkes, 107; Starkie, *A Lady's Child*, 215–16; Macardle, "The Dublin Student."

Alexandra College Guild, which she soon came to support. The Guild members, who favoured modern social work rather than the religious charity work that had attracted nineteenth-century middle-class women, were especially interested in housing for the urban poor and worked with tenement dwellers in deprived areas of Dublin.[57]

The feminist movement gathered pace in Ireland as well as in England in the decade before World War I, and Dorothy was first exposed to feminism as a student in Dublin. She was aware that new educational and professional opportunities for women meant that she had other choices besides marriage and family open to her, such as a teaching and writing career. "The women's cause was advancing," she observed, and she and some of her fellow students "meant to be in the vanguard."[58] Militant as well as constitutional suffrage groups were active in Dublin during Dorothy's college years. The Irish Women's Franchise League, whose tactics to obtain votes for women were influenced by Emmeline Pankhurst's militant WSPU in England, was formed in 1908 by Hanna Sheehy Skeffington, later a friend of Dorothy's, and Margaret Cousins. In addition, there were other women's groups active in Dublin, such as Inghinidhe na hÉireann, a cultural nationalist group founded by Maud Gonne.[59]

Dorothy became a passionate cultural nationalist as a young woman in Dublin. By the end of her student years, she later recalled, "Ireland possessed my imagination and my heart." Her interest in the works of W.B. Yeats, Standish O'Grady, Lady Gregory, and other writers associated with the Irish revival drew her to cultural nationalism, and she met leading writers and nationalist activists in Dublin, such as George Russell and Maud Gonne MacBride, once she became a recognized playwright herself.[60] Russell, known as Æ, presided over a weekly salon that drew artists, intellectuals, and

---

57 O'Connor and Parkes, 69–76; Maryann Gialanella Valiulis, "Toward 'The Moral and Material Improvement of the Working Classes': the Founding of the Alexandra College Guild Tenement Company, Dublin, 1898," *Journal of Urban History*, vol. 23, no. 3 (March 1997), 295–314. Dorothy, in her will, left money to the Guild.
58 She recalled this in a speech given in 1952. Dorothy Macardle, *ACD Magazine*, vol. 11 (June 1952), 6–9.
59 Rosemary Cullen Owens, *Smashing Times: a History of the Irish Women's Suffrage Movement, 1889–1922* (Dublin: Attic Press, 1984), 23–7; Margaret Ward, *Maud Gonne: Ireland's Joan of Arc* (London: Pandora Press, 1990), 65–6.
60 Dorothy Macardle, Witness Statement, NAI BMH/457; Macardle, "The Dublin Student."

advanced nationalists, and it was at his salon during the latter stages
of World War I that Dorothy first heard Irish republican aspirations
openly discussed. Dorothy was essentially apolitical as an Alexandra
student during the prewar years, and hardly followed the Parliamentary
debates on the third Home Rule bill, introduced in 1912. Her education
at unionist-oriented Alexandra College unwittingly contributed to her
later political transformation. Her study of English literature exposed
her to English poets, such as Shelley and Byron, who advocated
freedom and justice and opposition to tyranny, and her work with the
Guild and exposure to social injustice in Dublin made her wonder if
Ireland would be better served by Home Rule.[61]

During her college years, Dorothy was actively involved in literary
and dramatic activities, enriching her formal study of English literature.
She wrote for the *Alexandra College Dublin Magazine*, and joined the
college's Literary Society.[62] She directed Alexandra students in "Aucassin
and Nicolette," a French medieval romance she adapted for the stage.[63]
In 1909, she completed the First University Examination in Arts,
gaining Second Honours in English.[64] Dorothy earned a First Honours
B.A. from the National University of Ireland in 1912, winning third
place in English Language and Literature. Her graduation day was
marred somewhat by "a crowd of rowdy young men," in the galleries
who dropped flour, soot, and firecrackers on the few female graduates
approaching the dais below to receive their diplomas.[65]

Dorothy won a scholarship to Alexandra College's Training
Department in 1912, earning a Dublin University Teacher's Diploma
two years later. The award of a scholarship highlighted Dorothy's
academic ability and her desire for independence and a challenging
career, despite the initial opposition of her mother.[66] Other single
women from similar backgrounds remained financially dependent on
their wealthy parents. The Training Department was created in 1905

---

61 Macardle, "Living with Maud Gonne," Broadcast Talk, RTÉ Written Archives,
   15 September 1956; Macardle, "The Dublin Student."
62 Dorothy Macardle, "The Elizabethan Lyric," *ACD Magazine*, vol. 4, no. 35
   (December 1909), 8–14; Macardle, "Garden Phantoms," *ACD Magazine*, vol. 5,
   no. 40 (June 1912), 39–40; Ibid.,89.
63 *ACD Magazine*, vol. 5, no. 41 (December 1912), 40–1.
64 *ACD Magazine*, vol. 4, no. 35 (December 1909), 39.
65 Dorothy Macardle, Mills College Commencement Address, 12 June, 1939. Copy
   in the Mills College Archive, Oakland, California.
66 *ACD Magazine*, vol. 5, no. 41 (December 1912), 44; *ACD Magazine*, vol. 5, no.
   45 (December 1914), 59; Macardle, "The Dublin Student."

to provide a recognized course that would enable students to comply with the 1903 Registration of Teachers legislation, and register with the English Board of Education. The predominantly middle-class Irish and British women who trained as teachers at colleges like Alexandra were prepared for careers in private girls' schools, rather than in national schools in which teachers drawn from less privileged backgrounds taught students from the lower-middle and working classes. The course of study was progressive and modern for the early twentieth century, and Dorothy and her fellow students attended lectures on teaching methodologies, ethics, educational theory, and psychology.[67] Dorothy, who had a lifelong interest in psychology, may have had her first exposure to this emerging discipline during her teacher-training course. Overall, her educational experience can be placed within the context of greater educational and career opportunities for middle-class and affluent women in the early twentieth century.

Dorothy's educational achievements would not have been universally regarded in a favourable light at the time, as many commentators proclaimed that higher education undermined a young woman's feminine appeal and left her unmarriageable. While marriage rates for college-educated women, most of whom came from the middle and upper-middle classes, were comparatively low, they did not differ significantly from the marriage rates of women from similar backgrounds who had not attended college.[68] There were several reasons why many female college graduates in the early twentieth century chose not to marry. Some, like Dorothy, prized their careers and independence and were reluctant to play a dependent role in marriage like their mothers. Minnie and Thomas Macardle's difficult relationship may have heightened Dorothy's concerns about marriage and made her wary of emotional attachments. Other women found fulfilling same-sex relationships during and after college. Dorothy never married, and whether or not she had any serious relationships with men remains uncertain. Instead, she had several relationships of an ambiguous nature with other women during her life.

Her fiction may also provide insights into why she never married. *The Seed Was Kind*, Dorothy's most autobiographical novel, hints that something disturbing may have happened in an intimate relationship when she was young. In the novel, Diony, an idealistic and

67  O'Connor and Parkes, 80.
68  Dyhouse, *Girls Growing Up in Late Victorian and Edwardian England*, 159–60.

serious young woman who resembles Dorothy, gives into sexual pressure made by an unstable man she does not love, and then feels violated and deeply depressed. However, when she relates what happened to the man she does love, he praises her selflessness and asks her to marry him, rather than rejecting her. She joyfully accepts his proposal and regains her self-respect. Diony's actions are justified as self-sacrifice, since she gave into the demands of a man who was suicidally depressed.[69] Some of Dorothy's other works of fiction feature intensely emotional women who have short, intense affairs with men who abandon rather than marry them.[70]

Dorothy, who had a lifelong interest in Shakespeare, welcomed the opportunity to live and work in Stratford-upon-Avon, England, after completing her education.[71] She had long been interested in the Shakespeare Festival held in Stratford each spring and summer.[72] Dorothy attended the Festival in 1913, and took part in establishing the annual Conference for Teachers of English, which would be held during the summer festivals. She lived in Stratford between 1914 and 1916, and, as secretary for the teachers' conference, worked on Shakespeare projects with Sir Frank Benson, the renowned actor-manager, and the town's mayor, Archibald Flower. Dorothy also edited several Shakespeare plays for English textbooks for schoolchildren. Her sister Mona, now a young woman interested in acting, spent time working with her in Stratford. Dorothy's time in Stratford was clouded by her growing disillusionment with England, which she once viewed as the champion of liberty and democracy. She was dismayed by some of the upper-class English people she encountered, who were intensely hostile to Ireland and Home Rule. While she met more sympathetic Englishmen and women at the Shakespeare Conferences, she felt that those in power in England failed to uphold ideals of freedom and justice when it came to Ireland, and that they would be only too willing to use force to prevent Irish self-determination.[73]

69  Dorothy Macardle, *The Seed Was Kind* (London: Peter Davies, 1944), 213–22.
70  For example, Nuala in "The Portrait of Róisín Dhu," Carmel in *Uneasy Freehold*, and Terka in *Dark Enchantment*.
71  Dorothy Macardle to the Director of Talks [BBC], BBC Written Archives Centre, 29 March 1957.
72  Dorothy Macardle, "The Shakespeare Festival," *ACD Magazine*, vol. 5, no. 39 (December 1911), 17–25. See also Ron Eagle, Felicia Hardison Londre, and Daniel J. Watermeier (eds.), *Shakespeare Companies and Festivals: An International Guide* (Westport, Conn.: Greenwood Press, 1995), 473–6, for the origins and early years of the Stratford Festival.
73  Dorothy Macardle to the Director of Talks, BBC Written Archives Centre, 29

Dorothy was in the theatre in Stratford when World War I broke out in August 1914.[74] Ireland at the time was on the verge of a civil war, as Unionists had formed the Ulster Volunteer Force in 1912 to resist Home Rule, and nationalists responded by forming the Irish Volunteers. The outbreak of war in Europe may have averted civil war in Ireland. The Macardles, like many other Irish families with Unionist or moderate Home Rule sympathies, favoured the war effort, which would ultimately claim about 50,000 Irish lives.[75] John Redmond, the leader of the Irish Parliamentary Party, urged Irishmen to enlist in the British Army to defend Belgium against German aggression, and to prove that Ireland was worthy of Home Rule, which was granted in 1914 but suspended for the duration of the war.[76] Thomas Macardle chaired the County Louth Recruiting Committee. His enthusiasm for recruiting was such that he and a recruiting party "unwisely perhaps, interrupted proceedings in the picture house only to be greeted with shouts and catcalls."[77] As a member of the Dundalk Chamber of Commerce, Thomas, along with his colleagues, "lobbied hard for war industries to be located in [Dundalk] but to no avail,"[78] and advertisements for the Macardle brewery during the war years stressed the popularity of its products with the military. Dorothy's brothers Kenneth and John enlisted and fought with the British Army in France, as did other young men from the commercial and landowning elite in Louth. Kenneth left San Francisco, where he had been working, for England, where he successfully applied for a

March 1957; Tremayne, 88. Frank Benson briefly referred to Dorothy and Mona in his memoirs when recounting the names of those he had worked with in the Stratford Festival until he broke with it in 1919. See Sir Frank Benson, *My Memoirs* (London: Ernest Benn Limited, 1930), 294. See also Dorothy Macardle, "The Riddle of England," Broadcast Talk, RTÉ Written Archives, 8 September 1956.

74  Dorothy Macardle to the Director of Talks, BBC Written Archives Centre, 29 March 1957.

75  A number of works on Ireland and World War I have been published since the 1980s. See, for example, David Fitzpatrick, ed., *Ireland and the First World War* (Dublin, 1986); Myles Dungan, *They Shall Not Grow Old: Irish Soldiers and the Great War* (Dublin: Four Courts Press, 1997); and Adrian Gregory and Senia Paseta, eds., *Ireland and the Great War: 'A War to Unite Us All?'* (Manchester: Manchester University Press, 2002). For another example of a wealthy Irish Catholic family with intense pro-British sympathies during World War I, see Starkie, *A Lady's Child*, 198–205.

76  Patrick Maume, *The Long Gestation: Irish Nationalist Life, 1891–1918* (New York: St Martin's Press, 1999), 147–9.

77  *Thom's Directory* (Dublin, 1921); Hall, 37.

78  Hall, 33.

commission. He served in the Manchester Regiment's 17th Battalion, while John served in the Royal Field Artillery.[79]

The Great War divided Irish society, and the women of Ireland were no less conflicted than the men. Dorothy was "with the Allies during the world war in sympathies,"[80] though little is known about her level of support for Irish involvement in World War I, or her activities in the early stages of the war, when she lived in England. Her sister Mona joined Queen Mary's Auxiliary Army Corps. A number of Irishwomen from Alexandra College and from Louth engaged in charity work, volunteered with the Red Cross, or served as army nurses in France. Upper class, mainly Protestant women dominated war-related volunteer work in Ireland, although Catholic women who supported John Redmond's Irish Party, such as Lady Bellingham of Louth, were involved in the Red Cross and war relief work as well.[81] One of Ireland's leading feminists, Hanna Sheehy Skeffington of the Irish Women's Franchise League, was a committed pacifist, but other Irish feminists supported the war and redirected their efforts from the suffrage campaign to voluntary war work. Cumann na mBan, a nationalist women's group which Dorothy would later join, included members who were strongly opposed to the war from the start. Support for the war waned in the aftermath of the 1916 Rising, as did the participation of Catholic nationalist women in war work.[82]

The Easter Rising commenced on 24 April 1916. Militant republicans from the Irish Volunteers and the Irish Republican Brotherhood, disillusioned with constitutional nationalism and the postponement of Home Rule, occupied key points in Dublin, including the General Post Office, where Patrick Pearse proclaimed an Irish republic. The outnumbered insurgents fought British troops for nearly a week, finally surrendering on 30 April. Almost one hundred women from Cumann na mBan, the women's auxiliary to the Irish Volunteers, and the Irish Citizen Army, linked with the labour movement, were

---

79  Hall, 35. Kenneth had worked at the Canadian Bank of Commerce in London, as well as in San Francisco. See WO 339/28290, National Archives, Kew.

80  Dorothy Macardle, *The Irish Republic*, 4th ed. (Dublin: Irish Press Ltd., 1951), 23.

81  Eileen Reilly, "Women and Voluntary War Work," in Adrian Gregory and Senia Peseta, eds., *Ireland and the Great War: 'A War to Unite Us All?'* (Manchester: Manchester University Press, 2002), 66–7; Hall, 32–3. See also Tom Burke, "The Other Women of 1916," *History Ireland*, vol. 14, no. 5 (September/October 2006), 8–9, for more on Voluntary Aid Detachments, or VADs. For Mona Macardle, see War Office 372/23, National Archives, Kew.

82  Reilly, "Women and Voluntary War Work," 67.

actively involved in the Rising, and many were arrested, including Constance Markievicz and Kathleen Lynn. Fifteen male insurgents were executed in May, and both men and women were imprisoned. Dorothy, by this time, was aware of many of the leaders from cultural nationalist circles, such as Patrick Pearse, Thomas MacDonagh, and Joseph Plunkett, who were among those executed. Her family was outraged by the Rising, particularly her father and her brother Kenneth, who attributed it to German backing and "the treacherous blood and imbalanced useless minds of the lower Irish."[83]

The Macardles were ultimately to face a severe test during the war.[84] On 9 July 1916, Second Lieutenant Kenneth Macardle was reported missing in France after the Battle of Montauban. Thomas Macardle, in Dundalk, contacted the War Office immediately, mentioning that his wife, Minnie, an invalid who lived in London, would be glad of any comforting news the War Office could provide. Thomas' brother, Dundalk solicitor Peter Macardle, sought help from an old family friend, Irish Party MP Patrick Brady, but Brady was unable to obtain more information from the War Office. Thomas and Dorothy then collaborated in the search for news of Kenneth's fate, as Minnie Macardle was unable to participate. Dorothy, now based at her mother's London home, contacted the War Office several times, and she and Thomas sought help from another MP, E.A. Strauss, as well as enquiry agencies working from casualty lists sent to hospitals and prisoner-of-war camps in Germany. The Macardles' experience of searching for a missing soldier relative, sometimes with the help of outside agencies such as the Red Cross, was widely shared during World War I, although many families never discovered their relative' ultimate fate.[85]

In October 1916, the Macardles heard from a Zurich-based information bureau that Kenneth had been killed in Trones Wood. He had been shot through the head when running for reinforcements in an area of heavy shelling. Dorothy asked the War Office to convey the news of Kenneth's death to the newspapers for the Roll of Honour.

83 Donal Hall, *World War I and Nationalist Politics in County Louth, 1914–1920* (Dublin: Four Courts Press, 2005), 39.

84 The following account has been reconstructed from information contained in WO 339/28290, National Archives, Kew. For more on Kenneth Macardle, see also MR1/3/2/6, MR3/26/168, Tameside Archive.

85 Jay Winter, *Sites of Memory, Sites of Mourning: The Great War in European Cultural History* (Cambridge: Cambridge University Press, 1995), 35–43.

In February 1917, after obtaining witness statements from two privates in the Manchester Regiment, the War Office stated that for official purposes, Kenneth Macardle's death had occurred on 10 July 1916, and offered their condolences to the Macardles. Kenneth's body was never recovered. One of the many Allied casualties of the devastating Battle of the Somme, his name was inscribed on the Thiepval monument in France.[86] Kenneth's death may have contributed to Dorothy's interest in Spiritualism and séances after the war, as many of the people in the interwar era who took part in séances were trying to communicate with relatives killed in the war. In addition, some of her fiction may have indirectly commented on the Great War, based on her own family's experience. Her 1925 play, *The Old Man*, may be a commentary on the sacrifice of the young in the name of nationalism during World War I, as well as during the Irish revolution.

Dorothy returned to live permanently in Ireland in 1917. The country had changed greatly in the aftermath of the 1916 Rising, and Dorothy was to undergo dramatic changes in her own life and outlook in the years to come.

---

86  WO339/28290; MR1/3/2/6, Tameside Archive.

CHAPTER TWO

# Teacher and Republican, 1917–1923

THE IRELAND THAT Dorothy returned to in 1917 was very
different from the prewar Ireland she had left several years
earlier. When Dorothy, now twenty-eight, walked through the
centre of Dublin to the Abbey Theatre, she could see evidence of the
destruction that remained from the 1916 Rising. The popular mood
had changed as well, since sympathy for advanced nationalism had
increased in the aftermath of the executions of the leaders of the
Rising. The Great War raged on with horrific consequences. Despite
the inauspicious times, the next few years were crucial in Dorothy's
social and political formation, and fundamentally shaped the outlook
she maintained for the rest of her life. She experienced success as a
teacher and playwright, formed lifelong friendships, and, despite her
unlikely background, became a republican.

Dorothy's interest in theatre led her to new friendships and
allowed her to move outside of the conventional social circles of her
youth. The Irish theatre world, centered in Dublin, functioned as an
important space for political dissidence between the 1890s and
1920s.[1] It was in the Irish drama and literary world that Dorothy
began to discover alternative perspectives to those instilled in her by
her pro-British family and educational background. Here she met
leading nationalist figures and became a committed republican herself,

---

1 For the political and ideological aspects of the Irish theatre, see Ben Levitas, *The
Theatre of Nation: Irish Drama and Cultural Nationalism, 1890–1916* (Oxford:
Clarendon Press, 2002).

embracing the ideal of Irish independence rather than home rule.[2] Other forms of political dissidence, such as feminism and socialism, were also represented among the actors, directors, and dramatists.

The Abbey Theatre, founded in 1904 by W.B. Yeats and Lady Gregory, had played a pivotal role in the growth of Irish cultural nationalism in the decade preceding World War I, and retained its central role as a Dublin cultural and political institution. Dorothy had attended plays at the Abbey since her student days at Alexandra, and knew some of the theatre's leading figures. She met W.B. Yeats, at the time an outspoken nationalist as well as a poet and playwright, and Maud Gonne MacBride, Yeats' muse. MacBride was a tall, striking woman with a flamboyant personality. The daughter of a British army officer, she wholeheartedly embraced Irish cultural and political nationalism in her youth. In 1900, she founded the nationalist women's group Inghinidhe na hÉireann, which by 1915 became affiliated with Cumann na mBan. She had occasionally acted in plays, but also participated in street theatre on behalf of nationalism, and she and other members of the Inghinidhe staged political demonstrations. MacBride was a key influence in Dorothy's transformation into a nationalist, and the two became good friends and political associates.[3]

Edward Martyn also played an influential role in Dorothy's life at this time. The founder of the Irish Theatre, Martyn was also a playwright and the first president of Sinn Féin. Joseph Plunkett and Thomas MacDonagh were the co-directors of the Irish Theatre until 1916, when the two signatories of the Proclamation were executed for their role in the Rising. Dorothy greatly admired Edward Martyn and his theatre, which he founded in a disused schoolhouse on Hardwicke Street in a deprived area of Dublin's North Side. Like Dorothy, Martyn was an Irish nationalist with an appreciation of European culture. His art theatre, which lasted from 1914 to 1920, performed the works of modern European playwrights, mostly Scandinavian and Russian, for small audiences. Martyn favoured the plays of Hendrik Ibsen and Anton Chekov;[4] Dorothy, who first saw Chekov's plays performed at the Hardwicke Street theatre, preferred

2 Dorothy Macardle, Statement by Witness, NAI BMH/457.
3 Margaret Ward, *Maud Gonne: Ireland's Joan of Arc* (London: Pandora Press, 1990); Dorothy Macardle, Statement by Witness, NAI BMH/457.
4 William J. Feeney, *Drama in Hardwicke Street: A History of the Irish Theatre Company* (London and Toronto: Associated University Presses, 1984), 25, 36–9, 97–9.

Chekov to Ibsen. She appreciated the encouragement Martyn gave to emerging playwrights, and enjoyed bringing friends to "his little theatre in the city slums" to watch "the cheap serge curtain ... rise on Chekov's greatest play."[5] The Irish Theatre was undercut by the formation of the Dublin Drama League in 1918, initiated by W.B. Yeats and Lennox Robinson of the Abbey Theatre.[6]

A third link between theatre and politics could be found in Countess Constance Markievicz, who was involved in the Independent Theatre Company and the Dublin Repertory Theatre. She fought in the 1916 Rising with the Irish Citizen Army, and presided over the women's organization, Cumann na mBan. Dorothy became friendly with the Countess, and later joined Cumann na mBan. Other politically active women involved in theatre whom Dorothy met at the time included Helena Molony, Blanaid Salkeld, Daisy Bannard Cogley, and Móirín Chevasse. Molony was an Abbey actress and member of the Irish Citizen Army, Salkeld and Cogley acted in the Irish Theatre, and Chevasse was a playwright associated with the Irish Theatre.[7]

Dorothy, in 1917, began working on her own first play, *Asthara*, which premiered at Dublin's Little Theatre on 24 May 1918. The verse play was a fantasy set in the distant past, but its theme of renewal and transformation was especially timely in the context of Ireland after the 1916 Rising.[8] The protagonists were Asthara, played by Elizabeth Young, who had previously performed in Ibsen's plays, and Thorgyn, played by Paul Farrell, who acted with the Irish Theatre and belonged to the Irish Volunteers. Dorothy became close to Farrell, another crucial influence in recruiting her to the nationalist movement, at this time.[9] Thorgyn was "a superman, who prefers

5 Dorothy Macardle, "The Passing of Edward Martyn," *Sinn Féin*, 29 December 1923.

6 Feeney, *Drama in Hardwicke Street*, 232.

7 Levitas, *The Theatre of Nation*, 102, 207; Sinéad McCoole, *No Ordinary Women: Irish Female Activists in the Revolutionary Years, 1900–1923* (Dublin: O'Brien Press, 2003), 185–6; Dorothy Macardle File, Alexandra College Dublin; Feeney, *Drama in Hardwicke Street*, 52, 101–3, 189, 266–8. Cogley was in prison with Dorothy, while Salkeld and Chevasse later belonged to the Irish Women Writers' Club. For Cogley, see RJD, NLI MS 32,582 (43), 12 February 1923. For Chevasse, see her obituary in the *Irish Times*, 11 May 1972.

8 *ACD Magazine*, vol. 6, no. 52 (June 1918); Lelia Doolan, "Emblems of Adversity: Women in the Abbey Theatre," unpublished paper in possession of the author. There appear to be no existing scripts of this unpublished play.

9 Feeney, *Drama in Hardwicke Street*, 143, 175; Dorothy Macardle, "The Riddle of England," Broadcast Talk, RTÉ Written Archives, 8 September 1956.

2. Dorothy Macardle,
late 1920s.
(Source: Bulmer Hobson,
*The Gate Theatre*,
Dublin, 1934)

life's adventures to the wine of spirit life distilled by a superwoman [Asthara], who in turn rails against her gods of nature and abandons herself to love."[10] The high-minded, spiritual Asthara is "obedient to the teachings of God until the strong-limbed Thorgyn came to teach her love."[11] The play's depiction of a woman grappling with high ideals in challenging circumstances would later appear in some of Dorothy's other works. While most reviewers found the dreamy, mystical play difficult to grasp, they praised the elevated language.[12] Young and Farrell were commended for their interpretations of their roles. Mona Macardle, Dorothy's younger sister, played Asthara's follower, Úna, and did not fare as well with the critics. Her performance greatly irritated the *Irish Times* reviewer, who felt "her shivering monotone was a hindrance rather than a help to creating a mystic impression."[13]

Dorothy's three-act play, *Atonement*, premiered at the Abbey Theatre on 17 December 1918. It was her first play to engage the

10  "The Little Theatre," *Irish Times*, 25 May 1918, 5.
11  Robert Hogan and Richard Burnham, *The Art of the Amateur: 1916–1920* (Dublin: Dolmen Press, 1984), 164.
12  *Irish Times*, 25 May 1918, 5. See also Hogan and Burnham, 163–4.
13  *Irish Times*, 25 May 1918, 5.

theme of family violence, a theme that would run through her later plays and novels. *Atonement* signaled Dorothy's participation in an important Irish theatrical tradition; Irish drama "showed explicit scenes of violence as the familial norm," with *The Playboy of the Western World* as one of the most famous examples.[14] *Atonement* took place in contemporary rural Ireland, and centered on a violent dispute between neighboring families, the Farrahers and the Huggards. Young Shawn Farraher (played by Fred O'Donovan), who has returned home from America, seeks revenge on the elderly Daniel Huggard (Fred Harford), whom he suspects of killing his father. Donagh Huggard (Arthur Shields), Daniel's son and the fiancé of Shawn's sister Bridie (Columba O'Carroll), tries to protect his father from Shawn. The elder Huggard draws a gun, and, attempting to shoot at Shawn, kills his son Donagh instead. The play concludes with a devastated Bridie mourning the death of her fiancé. An *Irish Times* reviewer praised the acting and the plotting, but wondered "whether in the wildest districts the crime which forms the mainspring of the piece would have to clamour for such a personal vengeance as is attempted."[15] Other critics also found the play unrealistic, and one commented on the conventional, stereotyped characterizations. Rather than being original, the characters in *Atonement* were simply members of "the Gallery of Family Portraits in the Abbey repertory."[16] A later commentator, however, described the play as "an Ibsenite family drama of passion," noting that it could be seen as a precursor to later plays by T.C. Murray, Teresa Deevy, and Eugene McCabe.[17] After the play, to Dorothy's delight, W.B. Yeats encouraged her to write more plays, gave advice on building suspense, and invited her to tea at the home he was renting from Maud Gonne MacBride, whom Dorothy met the following year.[18]

By 1919, Dorothy was more involved in Cumann na mBan, the women's auxiliary of the Irish Volunteers. The organization had been formed in 1914 at the time of the Home Rule Crisis, and some members had taken part in the 1916 Rising. During the War of Independence,

14  Gerardine Meaney, "The Sons of Cúchulainn: Violence, the Family, and the Irish Canon," *Éire-Ireland* 41:1 & 2, Spring/Summer 2006, 252.

15  *Irish Times*, 18 December 1918, 3.

16  Robert Hogan and Richard Burnham, *The Art of the Amateur: 1916–1920* (Dublin: Dolmen Press, 1984), 151–2.

17  Lelia Doolan, "Emblems of Adversity: Women and the Abbey Theatre," unpublished paper in author's possession.

18  Dorothy Macardle, "Living with Maud Gonne," Broadcast Talk, RTÉ Written Archives, 15 September 1956.

Cumann na mBan worked in conjunction with the IRA. Dorothy joined the organization after Countess Markievicz's release from prison and subsequent reelection as president of Cumann na mBan. Under Markievicz's leadership, Cumann na mBan reorganized as part of the general regrouping of advanced nationalist organizations in 1917, when participants in the Easter Rising were released from prison. Membership in the organization increased dramatically during 1918. As a Cumann na mBan member, Dorothy was trained in first aid, propaganda, and information gathering. She distributed leaflets and took part in relief work, such as dispensing aid to the wives and families of political prisoners.

Dorothy was both typical and atypical of members of Cumann na mBan. Like most of the rank and file members, she was relatively young, single, Catholic, and self-supporting. While most of the young employed women worked in factories, offices, and shops, Dorothy, in contrast, was a university-educated teacher.[19] She differed from many Cumann na mBan members in that she came from a wealthy family with no republican connections. However, there were a few other prominent republican women whose backgrounds were also atypical. Countess Markievicz had been raised in an aristocratic Irish Protestant family in Sligo, and Maud Gonne MacBride came from a wealthy English Protestant family with British Army connections. Both women became Catholics. The Gifford sisters had been raised as Protestants in a religiously mixed Unionist family in Dublin, and like Dorothy had attended Alexandra College. Another Alexandra College graduate with a Protestant and Unionist background involved in Cumann na mBan was Kathleen Lynn, a doctor with socialist sympathies who had participated in the 1916 Rising as a member of the Irish Citizen Army.[20] Atypical members of Cumann na mBan, like Dorothy, became estranged from their families, who strongly opposed their republican politics.

Cumann na mBan members played an important role in opposing conscription for Ireland in spring 1918. The British government, responding to difficulties on the Western Front, sought to impose

---

19 Dorothy Macardle File, Alexandra College, Dublin; Sinéad McCoole, *No Ordinary Women*, 28–31, 64–8; Aideen Sheehan, "Cumann na mBan, Policies and Activities," in David Fitzpatrick, ed., *Revolution? Ireland 1917–1923* (Dublin: Leinster Leader Ltd, 1990), 88–97.

20 McCoole, *No Ordinary Women*, 166–86. See also Margaret Ó hÓgartaigh, *Kathleen Lynn: Irishwoman, Patriot, Doctor* (Dublin: Irish Academic Press, 2006).

conscription on Ireland in addition to raising the age of conscription in Britain. Cumann na mBan members took part in a day-long women's protest and canvassed for signatures on petitions to oppose conscription. Sinn Féin and other advanced nationalist groups were also instrumental in defeating conscription, and the protest was backed by the Catholic Church. Although John Redmond and other members of the Irish Parliamentary Party, who had originally supported the war and urged Irishmen to enlist, joined in the opposition to conscription, Sinn Féin reaped the political benefits of the anti-conscription protest. When elections were held in December 1918, a month after World War I ended, Sinn Féin candidates won most of the seats, and the Irish Parliamentary Party was drastically reduced. The December 1918 elections were the first elections in which women could run for office and vote, and Countess Markievicz successfully ran for Parliament. She and other Sinn Féin candidates, however, did not take their seats in Parliament, in keeping with their abstentionist policy. They established the First Dáil in Dublin as an alternative elected Parliament,[21] and the stage was set for a new episode in Anglo-Irish relations.

At about this time, Dorothy met the man who was to become the central political influence in her life, and whose impact on twentieth-century Ireland was profound as well. Dorothy joined Sinn Féin,[22] which like other nationalist organizations began to regroup after the Rising, and became intrigued by the tall, gaunt, dark-haired man who was elected Sinn Féin's president in 1917. Éamon de Valera, whose remote and ascetic manner appealed to Dorothy, had joined the Irish Volunteers in 1912, and in 1916 commanded the Boland's Mills battalion in the southeastern part of Dublin. De Valera was spared execution for his role in the 1916 Rising, instead serving a year-long prison term. His links with the executed leaders of the 1916 Rising enhanced his credibility as the leader of the advanced nationalist movement. By late 1917, he was the president of the Irish Volunteers as well as of Sinn Féin, and thus gained control of the military as well as the political side of the radical nationalist movement. As Sinn Féin's president, he committed the organization to "securing the international recognition of Ireland as an independent republic." Sinn Féin declared its rejection of the British government's right to rule

21 McCoole, *No Ordinary Women*, 66–70.
22 Dorothy Macardle File, Alexandra College, Dublin.

Ireland, and discussed establishing an alternative elected government in Dublin which would then direct resistance to British rule.[23]

Dorothy's professional life took a turn when she was appointed to the Pfeiffer Lectureship in English at Alexandra College in 1918, an atypical occupation for a republican activist. The college was still a bastion of Unionism, so Dorothy was politically at odds with most of her colleagues and students.[24] The lectureship was named after Emily Pfeiffer, "a poet and feminist who [left] a substantial trust for the promotion of higher education for women."[25] Dorothy approached her teaching responsibilities with great enthusiasm, and especially enjoyed teaching Shakespeare, the Romantic poets, and W.B. Yeats. She became friendly with her students, and many of them found her an outstanding teacher and a charismatic figure. "Dorothy Macardle was by far the most stimulating teacher I have ever had," one former student recalled years later. Another was struck by the tall, thin woman with the "pale bony face, heavy-lidded eyes and an expression of burning intensity." Dorothy read poetry aloud in a musical voice as she absentmindedly smoothed her long brown hair, which she wore parted on the side and pulled back into an upsweep.[26]

Dorothy moved from an Ely Place flat to 73 St Stephen's Green, the home of Maud Gonne MacBride, in the autumn of 1920. During her years as a teacher, she often invited students home for tea and literary discussions. She advised students on their own drama productions at the college, and took them to plays at the Abbey Theatre and to Shakespearean productions at the Gaeity Theatre.[27] She produced W.B. Yeats' play *The Countess Cathleen* at Alexandra in May 1922, and the rehearsals were particularly memorable for the students involved in the production.[28] Dorothy invited her English Literature

23 Pauric Travers, *Éamon de Valera* (Dundalk: Dundalgan Press, 1994), 6–14; Dorothy Macardle, *The Irish Republic* (Dublin: Irish Press, 4th ed), 232–3.
24 *ACD Magazine*, vol. 6, no. 54 (June 1919), 284; Anne V. O'Connor and Susan M. Parkes, *Gladly Learn and Gladly Teach: Alexandra College and School, 1866–1966* (Dublin: Blackwater Press, 1984), 109.
25 Maxine Berg, *A Woman in History: Eileen Power, 1889–1940* (Cambridge: Cambridge University Press, 1996), 76.
26 O'Connor and Parkes, 109. Dorothy, aged thirty, is pictured with fellow teachers in a 1919 staff photograph. She wears the Tara brooch worn by Inghinidhe na hÉireann members. O'Connor and Parkes, 96.
27 E.R.F., "Dorothy Macardle," *ACD Magazine*, vol. 11, no. 128 (June 1959). See also Mary Manning, "The Schoolgirls of Alexandra," *Irish Times*, 3 June 1978.
28 *ACD Magazine*, vol. 7 (June 1922) 19. See also E.R.F., "Dorothy Macardle," *ACD Magazine*, vol. 11 (June 1959); Mary Manning, "The Schoolgirls of Alexandra,"

students to Maud Gonne MacBride's house for rehearsals, and they were delighted that Yeats came to the last rehearsal and offered advice on their acting.[29] Some of Dorothy's students later became successful in the theatre world. Mary Manning became a dramatist whose plays were produced at the Gate Theatre in the 1930s, while Shelagh Richards became an actress at the Gate.

Republican political activity began to take up more of Dorothy's time when the War of Independence broke out in January 1919. The Dáil, the alternative government comprised of successful Sinn Féin candidates who refrained from taking their seats in Parliament, met in Dublin on 21 January 1919, the same day an ambush by the Irish Republican Army took place in Tipperary. The IRA carried out arms raids and engaged in guerrilla warfare against the British forces; their goal was a fully independent republic, rather than Home Rule.[30] Dorothy became involved in relief work and in publicity, helping Maud Gonne MacBride set up the White Cross to help civilians in early 1921. This republican-oriented organization provided relief to Irish civilians suffering deprivation as a result of the war, and publicized atrocities by the British forces, particularly the Black and Tans, an auxiliary force. Dorothy lived through night-time raids by the Black and Tans, who searched the MacBride house for Maud's son Seán, an IRA member. The White Cross generated cross-community support, with many Quakers involved.[31] Dorothy, through her investigative journalism and publicity work for the White Cross, became close to Erskine Childers of the Sinn Féin Publicity Bureau, who ran the *Irish Bulletin* following the arrest of the republican paper's first editor, Desmond FitzGerald, in 1921.

Dorothy lived almost a double life at this time, teaching at Unionist-oriented Alexandra College and working for Irish independence.

*Irish Times*, 3 June 1978. Ironically, this play was disliked by Irish nationalists. See P.J. Mathews, *Revival: The Abbey Theatre, Sinn Féin, the Gaelic League, and the Co-operative Movement* (Cork: Cork University Press, 2003), 35–65.

29  E.R.F., "Dorothy Macardle," *ACD Magazine*, vol. 11, no. 128 (June 1959); Mary Manning, "The Schoolgirls of Alexandra," *Irish Times*, 3 June 1978; Anne V. O'Connor and Susan M. Parkes, *Gladly Learn and Gladly Teach: Alexandra College and School, 1866–1966* (Dublin: Blackwater Press, 1984), 109, 115.

30  Michael Hopkinson, *The Irish War of Independence* (Dublin: Gill and Macmillan, 2002), 38, 115.

31  Dorothy Macardle, Statement by Witness NAI BMH/457; Dorothy Macardle of the White Cross, Dublin Committee to the Honorary Secretary, Friends Relief Sub-Committee, Religious Society of Friends Historical Library, Dublin, MSS Box 69, Folder 3, 12 April 1921; *Report of the Irish White Cross to 31st August 1922* (Dublin: Martin Lester, 1922); Macardle, "Living with Maud Gonne."

Students and teachers at Alexandra were aware that Dorothy was involved in Sinn Féin and revolutionary activities. The principal, Miss White, warned her that she could lose her job, and Dorothy promised to keep politics out of her classroom. In the autumn of 1920, she befriended Cumann na mBan activist Máire Comerford, who also moved to St Stephen's Green South at that time. Comerford became the secretary to Alice Stopford Green, a nationalist historian involved in Cumann na mBan and the White Cross.[32] Dorothy also became friendly with Green's niece, Dorothy Stopford, a republican doctor who worked with the IRA brigades in Cork. The IRA leader Michael Collins sometimes hid out at 90 St Stephen's Green, and the house was raided several times by the Black and Tans.[33] Linda Kearns, another new friend of Dorothy's, also provided a safe house for IRA men in Dublin, and served as a spy for Collins. Kearns, who was arrested in 1920 for smuggling weapons, was a republican nurse from Sligo who gave talks on first aid at Cumann na mBan meetings.[34]

In December 1920, Dorothy and her friends Maud Gonne MacBride, Rosamond Jacob, Hanna Sheehy Skeffington, and Kathleen Lynn attended the court martial of Countess Markievicz at the Royal Barracks. Markievicz, head of Cumann na mBan, had also founded the Fianna, a boy scout organization whose members went on to join the IRA. Thus, Markievicz was tried and imprisoned for high treason because the Fianna, as a source of recruits for the IRA, was implicated in the killing of British troops.[35] Shortly after the Countess' court martial, Dorothy headed to London to meet with Margot Asquith and ask for her help in appealing for a reprieve in the death sentence of a young Irishman.[36] While in England, Dorothy also met with Charlotte Despard, a feminist, socialist, and pacifist, as well as the sister of Lord French, the Viceroy of Ireland, which enhanced her

---

32  O'Connor and Parkes, 146; Macardle, "Living With Maud Gonne"; Manning, "The Schoolgirls of Alexandra;" McCoole, *No Ordinary Women*, 150. Alice Stopford Green's house was at 90 St Stephen's Green South.

33  León Ó Bróin, *Protestant Revolutionaries in Ireland: the Stopford Connection* (Dublin: Gill and MacMillan, 1985), 167–8, 173–4; Nadia Clare Smith, *A 'Manly Study'? Irish Women Historians, 1868–1949* (Basingstoke and New York: Palgrave Macmillan, 2006), 65–6.

34  Sinéad McCoole, *No Ordinary Women*, 177.

35  RJD, NLI MS 32,582 (38), 2 December 1920.

36  Ward, 123–4. Asquith and other influential political figures lobbied the Prime Minister, David Lloyd George, and the Irishman's life was spared. Máire Comerford, unpublished autobiography, UCDA LA18/23.

status as a witness and publicist of Black and Tan atrocities. Dorothy told Despard of the tactical differences within Sinn Féin and expressed the fear of "something desperate [by the IRA], then a massacre, followed by a stifling of all spirit." She convinced Despard to return to Ireland with her for a fact-finding tour with the intent of publicizing the suffering of Irish civilians to British audiences. A few months later, Despard joined Dorothy and Maud Gonne MacBride on a fact-finding mission to Balbriggan, where houses and a factory had been destroyed by the Black and Tans in September 1920. A picture shows the three women in Balbriggan, with MacBride and Despard in their usual widow's weeds and the much younger Dorothy, then thirty-two, in a hat and long, light-colored coat.[37] Dorothy's humanitarian work with victims of violence in Ireland foreshadowed her later investigative journalism and human rights advocacy in postwar Europe.

The IRA and the British forces reached a truce on July 11, 1921, and peace treaty negotiations between Michael Collins and David Lloyd George in London soon followed. The Government of Ireland Act of 1920 had partitioned Ireland and established parliaments in Dublin and Belfast. The Anglo-Irish Treaty, signed in December 1921, fell short of the republican aspiration for complete Irish independence. Northern Ireland retained political links with Britain, while the Irish Free State, with a Parliament in Dublin, achieved dominion status. Dorothy, who was now inclined to be influenced by her political hero, Sinn Féin president Éamon de Valera, as well as the republican journalist Erskine Childers, had reservations about the Treaty. While supporters of the new Free State argued that the Treaty settlement could be a steppingstone to full independence, many committed republicans like Dorothy were unconvinced by this argument, and watched with dismay as the Free State government ratified the Treaty in January 1922. Deputies who opposed ratification, led by Éamon de Valera, left the Dáil and began to strategize. Dorothy attributed her "intense anti-Treaty feeling" to the zeal of a convert to republicanism; "like most converts to a cause, [she] was zealous to the point of fanaticism."[38] She attended the Cumann na mBan conven-

---

37  Ward, 123–4; Margaret Mulvihill, *Charlotte Despard: A Biography* (London: Pandora Press, 1989), 7–8; Máire Comerford, unpublished autobiography, UCDA LA18/23.
38  Dorothy Macardle, Witness Statement, NAI BMH/457.

tion of February 1922, where members reaffirmed their opposition to the Anglo-Irish Treaty and their commitment to republicanism.[39]

She continued to write plays, and on 6 April 1922, her historical play *Ann Kavanagh* was produced at the Abbey.[40] *Ann Kavanagh*, which takes place in Wexford during the 1798 Rising, dealt with a woman who has to choose between saving a fugitive informer and demonstrating loyalty to her republican husband and his fellow insurgents, who plan to hunt down and execute the informer. The play generated an enthusiastic response from the audience, and drama reviewers praised the construction of the play and the acting of May Craig, as Ann, and of P.J. Carolan, who played Ann's husband Myles. Critics later commented on the apparent incongruity of the republican Dorothy Macardle objecting to Seán O'Casey's *The Plough and the Stars* in 1926, when both *Ann Kavanagh* and *The Plough and the Stars* "made the point that an allegiance to general humanity was more important than an allegiance to patriotism."[41] The play's theme of divided loyalties resonated with Dorothy's own experience. Ann Kavanagh, raised a Protestant and a loyalist, now identifies with Catholics and republicans, while Dorothy, a republican, was originally a unionist and had pro-British family members who objected to her politics.[42] Political commitments, she knew from personal experience, could tear couples and families apart.

Erskine Childers established a newspaper called *An Phoblacht*, or *The Republic*, in January 1922, and Dorothy soon joined his staff. Childers, in his paper, wrote about the limitations of the Treaty and urged Irishmen and women to continue to hold out for a sovereign, fully independent republic. Dorothy headed to Belfast in early June to report on the plight of Catholic civilians for *An Phoblacht*. The IRA was still active there, and the Northern Irish government had established a Special Constabulary with extensive powers. Civilians from the minority Catholic nationalist community in Belfast were in an especially vulnerable position. Many were burned out of their homes and driven out of their neighbourhoods by Unionists who felt they

39 Sinéad McCoole, *No Ordinary Women*, 87–9. A photograph taken at the convention shows Dorothy with, among others, Countess Markievicz and Leslie Barry. McCoole, 87.
40 Robert Hogan and James Burnham, *The Years of O'Casey: 1921–1926* (Dublin: Dolmen Press, 1992), 75–77.
41 Robert Hogan and Richard Burnham, *The Years of O'Casey: 1921–1926* (Dublin: Dolmen Press, 1992), 77.
42 Lelia Doolan, "Emblems of Adversity," 9.

could act with impunity. Between January and June 1922, 171 Catholics and 93 Protestants were killed in Northern Ireland. Dorothy witnessed disturbing scenes in a Belfast hospital following an attack on a Catholic area of Belfast in early June by heavily armed Special Constables, apparently in reprisal for an IRA attack on the Specials. "Even the children's wards," she wrote, "were filled with bullet wound and shrapnel-wound victims." One night, "the hospital was surrounded by an armed mob that fired through the windows with rifles and revolvers."[43]

The Irish Civil War broke out on 28 June 1922, when the Free State Army launched an assault on the Four Courts, which had been taken over by the republican dissidents. Dorothy woke up to the sounds of bombardment, and made her way to Erskine Childers. He encouraged Dorothy and other republican journalists to keep up their publicity work.[44] The fall of the Four Courts occurred on 30 June and the next major confrontation between the Free State troops and the IRA's Dublin Brigade took place on O'Connell Street. Dorothy was relieved by the IRA's surrender at the Four Courts, as it averted greater loss of life.[45] Several buildings on O'Connell Street, including the Hammam Hotel, were held by a small garrison led by Cathal Brugha. The garrison surrendered to the Free State forces on 5 July, but Brugha emerged from the hotel firing revolvers, and was shot by Free State troops. Dorothy's friend Linda Kearns, the nurse and republican activist, was with Brugha when he was wounded, and he died two days later. Cumann na mBan women were involved in the Civil War at the outset, acting as nurses, propagandists, message carriers, and providers of safe houses for the IRA. They played a larger role in the Civil War than in the War of Independence, and were subjected to mass arrests for their activities.[46]

Dublin was now under the control of the Free State government. The IRA was strongest in rural areas of Munster, Ireland's southernmost province, where it operated as a guerrilla force against the Free State troops until 1923. Erskine Childers left Dublin in July 1922 to

43  Dorothy Macardle, *The Irish Republic,* 4th ed. (Dublin: Irish Press Ltd., 1951), 658, 728–9; Macardle, Statement by Witness, NAI BMH/457.
44  Dorothy Macardle, "A Year Ago," *Éire,* 14 July 1923, 2.
45  Macardle, "A Year Ago," *Éire,* 14 July 1923, 2.
46  Dorothy Macardle, *The Irish Republic,* 4th ed. (Dublin: Irish Press Ltd., 1951), 745–54; McCoole, *No Ordinary Women,* 90–3; Sheehan, "Cumann na mBan," 93–7.

travel south to the "Munster Republic" with Éamon de Valera, Robert Brennan, and de Valera's secretary Kathleen O'Connell. Dorothy joined their group as a journalist for *An Phoblacht*, and spent some time that summer working in Waterford.[47] In August, the Free State leader Michael Collins was assassinated in Cork. By autumn, Dorothy had returned to Dublin and was working for the Republican Publicity Department, producing a newspaper called *Irish Freedom* in conjunction with Countess Markievicz, as well as teaching at Alexandra College. Dorothy also worked on behalf of IRA prisoners and their dependants with Maud Gonne MacBride, and spoke at public meetings of the Women's Prisoners' Defence League, founded by MacBride and Charlotte Despard.[48]

On 9 November 1922, Dorothy was arrested at the Suffolk Street headquarters of Sinn Féin. The Suffolk Street building had been raided by Free State troops, and Daisy Bannard Cogley, Lily O'Brennan, Kathleen O'Carroll, and others besides Dorothy were incarcerated in Mountjoy, an old jail on the North Side of Dublin.[49] Dorothy's apartment in the MacBride house was vandalized shortly afterwards, and many of her papers were destroyed by the Free State soldiers.[50]

Mary MacSwiney, a Cumann na mBan member from Cork, went on hunger strike in Mountjoy in November as a "protest against foreign domination in Ireland."[51] Dorothy helped nurse her friend and publicize MacSwiney's dire situation. She and fifteen other women signed a letter to the *Nation* on 18 November in which they compared Mary with her brother, Terence MacSwiney, who had starved himself to death in Brixton Prison in 1920, during the War of Independence. "Irishmen and women!" the signatories wrote. "Will you allow the sister of Terence MacSwiney to die for you in an Irish Gaol?"[52] MacSwiney's case gained widespread publicity, and she was released at the end of November, when she was near death.[53] Dorothy admired her friend intensely. "If I am kept here a year," she

47　Robert Brennan, *Allegiance* (Dublin: Browne and Nolan, 1950), 347–8.
48　Dorothy Macardle, Statement by Witness, NAI BMH/457; RJD, NLI MS 32,582 (42), 1 November 1922.
49　*Poblacht na h-Éireann War News*, no. 90, 11 November 1922.
50　RJD, NLI MS 32,582 (42), 11 November 1922.
51　Charlotte Fallon, "Civil War Hungerstrikes: Women and Men," *Éire-Ireland*, vol. 22 (1987), 77.
52　Dorothy Macardle, Statement by Witness, NAI BMH/457; *Nation*, 18 November 1922, 2–3.
53　Fallon, "Civil War Hungerstrikes," 76–9; Oonagh Walsh, "Testimony From Imprisoned Women," in David Fitzpatrick, ed., *Revolution? Ireland 1917–23*

told MacSwiney, "I shall still be as thankful as I am tonight that fate brought me here and gave me the proud and blessed privilege of being near you through [the hunger strike] … I think it will all work the miracle for Ireland."[54] While MacSwiney survived and won release from prison, Dorothy was devastated when another of her close friends, Erskine Childers, met his death that November when he was executed by Free State troops.[55]

Rosamond Jacob, who met Dorothy in 1920, was arrested in Hanna Sheehy Skeffington's house on 30 December 1922.[56] During her short incarceration in Mountjoy, she came to know Dorothy, with whom she shared a cell, and found her "a very responsive person to talk to, and interested in what you tell of your mind." Dorothy took part in debates and concerts, and Jacob found that she also wrote stories and plays.[57] While Jacob liked her, Dorothy's presence generated mixed reactions among the other republican women prisoners. According to Daisy Cogley, who had first met her in the Irish Theatre, Dorothy was widely disliked by the "Suffolk Street" women, linked by their connection with the Suffolk Street headquarters of Sinn Féin, where most were arrested. Cogley gave Jacob "a fearful account of the instinctive objection of Suffolk Street to Dorothy." They wanted her out. Jacob thought the source of their animosity was that Dorothy was "too unimpulsive" for them, and that she may have been seen as a weak link because she was less radical and unwilling to go along with all of Suffolk Street's plans to disrupt prison life by keeping up a "state of war." Cogley felt that she felt she should have been kinder to Dorothy, and her guilt about this made her dislike Dorothy more.[58]

Dorothy's father believed that a period of incarceration for Dorothy could do her a world of good. Sir Thomas Macardle, "a very genial elderly solid person" who had recently been knighted, visited Rosamond Jacob to discuss his daughter. Though concerned about her well-being, he felt a prison term would be beneficial for Dorothy because she had lived such an academic, cloistered life, associating primarily with

(Dublin, 1990), 69–85; Aideen Sheehan, "Cumann na mBan, Policies and Activities," in David Fitzpatrick, ed., *Revolution? Ireland 1917–23* (Dublin, 1990), 88–97.

54  Dorothy Macardle to Mary MacSwiney, Mary MacSwiney Papers, UCDA P48a/371 (4), Monday [27 November 1922].
55  Michael Hopkinson, *Green Against Green: The Irish Civil War* (Dublin: Gill and Macmillan, 1988) 189–90.
56  Rosamond Jacob Papers, NLI MS 33,125.
57  RJD, NLI MS 32,582 (43), 6–25 January 1923.
58  RJD, NLI MS 32,582 (43), 12 February 1923; McCoole, 100.

people similar to herself. He gave Jacob some money to give to Dorothy, and sent gifts to Dorothy in prison, some of which she shared with her fellow inmates.[59] Although he supported the Free State government and denounced republicanism,[60] he put politics aside to show his concern. He had some experience of republican prisoners by this time, as he had been a visiting justice to Dundalk Gaol, where he met with Austin Stack and other hunger-striking republican prisoners. Macardle did not want them to die, and convinced a Dublin Castle official to release them.[61]

In early 1923, Dorothy and other women were moved from Mountjoy to Kilmainham Gaol. Dorothy forged close friendships with some of her fellow prisoners in Kilmainham, despite the antagonism of much of Suffolk Street. She became friendly with Florence O'Byrne, Lily O'Brennan, Nora Connolly O'Brien, and Cecilia Gallagher.[62] Florence O'Byrne was involved with Sinn Féin, and, like Dorothy, was a relatively recent convert to republicanism.[63] Lily O'Brennan, a writer and participant in the Easter Rising, had been Erskine Childers' secretary. Nora Connolly O'Brien was the daughter of James Connolly, one of the executed leaders of the 1916 Rising, and a labour and republican activist herself. Cecilia Gallagher, who was considered apolitical, was the wife of Dorothy's friend Frank Gallagher, a leading republican journalist.[64] Dorothy, originally an English teacher, began teaching history in Kilmainham, offering a "Revolutionist Irish History" class three nights each week. In her class, her students learned "the old story of our history repeats itself in the warfare pursued by the English against us, and the political intrigues ... in the very old days just as now – and their pretended peace and conciliation schemes."[65] Although Dorothy's ties with Alexandra College had been severed by an official termination of her teaching position in December 1922,[66] one of the few nationalist students at Alexandra

59 RJD, NLI MS 32,582 (43), 4 February 1923.
60 RJD, NLI MS 32,582 (43), 14 February 1923; Dorothy Macardle, Statement by Witness, NAI BMH/457.
61 Donal Hall, *World War I and Nationalist Politics in County Louth, 1914–1920* (Dublin: Four Courts Press, 2005), 26.
62 O'Brennan Papers, UCDA P13/1, 22 February 1923.
63 RJD, NLI MS 32,582 (59), 19 January 1928.
64 McCoole, *No Ordinary Women*, 164.
65 O'Brennan Papers, P13/44, 14 March 1923.
66 At that time, the Council informed Dorothy and her father that she was being let go, as she was frequently absent and unable to carry out her teaching responsibilities. Dorothy Macardle File, Alexandra College.

made an effort to keep in touch with her in prison. Lilian Dalton, who was awarded the Pfeiffer English Scholarship in 1922, visited Rosamond Jacob to ask about Dorothy, and sent packages to her in prison.[67]

The prisoners commemorated the seventh anniversary of the Easter Rising and the subsequent executions of its leaders in April 1923. Dorothy felt it was especially meaningful to be in Kilmainham, where the leaders were executed, because the female prisoners were upholding the legacy of the 1916 Rising. The commemoration was heavily inflected with religiosity. The prisoners attended a morning mass, and later said the rosary and sang "Faith of Our Fathers." Some took the oath of allegiance to the Republic again. Speeches were made by women who were related to the executed leaders, such as Grace Gifford Plunkett, widow of Joseph Plunkett, and Nora Connolly, daughter of James Connolly. Dorothy seemed most moved by Nora Connolly reading the Proclamation of the Republic and her father's last statement, but overall, the speeches made it seem "as if the voices of our dead leaders were speaking to us again – no one who was here will forget." Dorothy and her comrades were saddened to think how devastated the men of 1916 would feel knowing "that their countrymen have betrayed them and desecrated their place of martyrdom," but were proud that they had received "a sacrament of confirmation in the republican faith."[68]

While Dorothy used the language and imagery of Catholic religious faith when discussing republicanism at this time, her own relationship to Catholicism was unraveling. She was deeply angered by the Catholic Church's excommunication of republicans during the Civil War.[69] She ceased to be identified as a Catholic, although her religious identity had not always been clear to people before or since. While she was sometimes perceived as a Protestant, from the 1920s onwards she was an agnostic who had severed all ties with the Catholic Church, rather than simply a lapsed or indifferent Catholic.[70]

Hunger strikes were continually resorted to by republican prisoners during the Civil War to attain political concessions or to force releases.[71]

---

67  RJD, NLI MS 32,582 (43), 28 February 1923. For Lilian Dalton (later Soiron), see *ACD Magazine*, vol. 7 (December 1922), 25; *ACD Magazine*, vol. 7 (December 1923), 32; Margaret Ward, *Maud Gonne: Ireland's Joan of Arc* (London: Pandora Press, 1990), 137.
68  Dorothy Macardle, "A Letter From Kilmainham," *Éire*, 12 May 1923, 5.
69  Tremayne, 91.
70  Ann Keating to author, 14 June 2004. Dorothy did not have a funeral Mass when she died in 1958.
71  Fallon, "Civil War Hungerstrikes," 76.

Some concessions were won by the women prisoners after a week-long hunger strike in late March, in which Dorothy participated.[72] Her involvement in the hunger strike drastically affected her already fragile health. A medical examination after her release showed she had spots on her lung, and a doctor initially feared she might not be able to live in Ireland due to the climate.[73] Mary MacSwiney, who had been arrested again, nearly died in late April after refusing to eat for almost three weeks. The other women prisoners in Kilmainham were to be removed to the North Dublin Union, but did not want to leave MacSwiney alone in Kilmainham. At the time of the planned removal, the prisoners, using a suffragette method[74] of resisting arrest, locked arms and massed themselves against the iron railings running the length of the top floor of the jail. The CID and the military police rushed into the jail to remove them by force. Several other women were beaten and removed before Dorothy was pulled away. As it was initially impossible for the police officers to make her lose her hold on the iron railings, they resorted to beating. She then felt "a great hand clos[ing] on [her] face, blinding and stifling [her]," and was thrown on the floor. She lost consciousness as she was dragged down the stairs. She and the other women were then loaded into lorries and driven to the NDU. The whole removal, she noted defiantly, "took five hours." Dorothy was ultimately spared a long stay in the NDU, where conditions were harsher than Kilmainham.[75] Due to her father's intervention, she was unconditionally released, on health grounds, shortly after the removal.[76]

The Civil War ended in late April, with the Free State army victorious and the republican side in disarray. When Dorothy returned to life outside prison, she was no longer just an atypical republican figure from a wealthy background, but someone on the losing side of a desperate war who had been imprisoned for the republic. It had been a long way from Dundalk and Alexandra College to Kilmainham Gaol.

72 O'Brennan Papers, UCDA, P13/1; McCoole, *No Ordinary Women*, 117–18. See also Dorothy Macardle, "Kilmainham Tortures: Experiences of a Released Prisoner," *Éire*, 26 May 1923, 5.
73 Dorothy Macardle to Owen Sheehy Skeffington, Sheehy Skeffington Papers, NLI MS 40,505 (5), 8 December 1937.
74 McCoole, *No Ordinary Women*, 122.
75 Dorothy Macardle, "Kilmainham Tortures," *Éire*, 26 May 1923, 5; McCoole, *No Ordinary Women*, 123–5.
76 RJD, NLI MS 32, 582 (44), 7 May 1923.

# CHAPTER THREE

# Journalism and Fianna Fáil, 1923–1931

D OROTHY BECAME A full-time writer and political activist in 1923, having lost her teaching position at Alexandra College during her imprisonment. While she remained a convinced republican who opposed the Free State government during the 1920s, she increasingly placed greater emphasis on using the political process to achieve republican goals by the end of the decade. She helped promote constitutional republicanism and the new Fianna Fáil party while continuing to forge a career as a journalist and playwright.

The Free State government, led by William Cosgrave of the Cumann na nGaedheal party, initiated the process of state consolidation in the early 1920s. New institutions were created, such as the Free State Army in 1922 and an unarmed police force, the Garda Síochána, in 1924. Cosgrave's administration was characterized by its fiscal conservatism and restricted social welfare expenditure, which limited its appeal among the urban and rural poor.[1] In the early years of the Free State, the Catholic Church, which embraced the great majority of the Free State's people, carved out a powerful social and political role for itself, contributing to the conservative social climate. Despite republican losses during the Civil War, Sinn Féin, the IRA, and Cumann na mBan still existed as potentially destabilizing forces in the Free State, and the government monitored their activities and

---

1 K. Theodore Hoppen, *Ireland Since 1800: Conflict and Conformity* (London: Longman, 1989), 174–80.

later passed repressive legislation directed at them.[2] Dorothy retained her ties with Sinn Féin and Cumann na mBan as these organizations, and the IRA, began to regroup in the aftermath of the Civil War.

She lived an unsettled existence for some time after her release in May 1923, and it would be two years before she established a permanent home. During the summer of 1923, Dorothy spent time in the glens of Wicklow before returning to Dublin.[3] She took lodgings at Frankfort House, a boarding house in Dartry owned by the Coghlans, a republican family. Countess Markievicz lived there as well during the 1920s. May Coghlan, the oldest Coghlan daughter, was a Cumann na mBan member who worked with the Countess and had been a prisoner in Kilmainham and the North Dublin Union.[4]

Although she was "profoundly depressed by what appeared to be the overthrow of the republican cause," Dorothy soon returned to political activity and investigative journalism, and contributed to several republican papers. With her "unlimited belief in the value of propaganda for the cause,"[5] she reported on the plight of republican prisoners in order to sway public opinion. Many other republican women remained incarcerated long after her release, and her friend Máire Comerford went on hunger strike. Dorothy felt Comerford's hunger strike would inspire Irish republicans to keep up the resistance to the Treaty and the Free State in the aftermath of the military collapse of the anti-Treaty forces. A woman allowed to starve herself to death in prison for her beliefs would be dramatic and powerful propaganda for the republican cause, and would destroy the moral credibility of the Free State government.[6] The republican spirit of suffering political prisoners could not be crushed, Dorothy warned; the Free State authorities would "learn their lesson very soon, learn that this war against the prisoners is as futile as any war ever waged by an enslaved and fool-ridden state."[7]

---

2  Brian Hanley, *The IRA, 1926–1936* (Dublin: Four Courts Press, 2002); Fearghal McGarry, *Frank Ryan* (Dundalk: Dundalgan Press, 2002).
3  RJD, NLI MS 32,582 (44), 2 July 1923.
4  Dorothy gave Frankfort House as her address at this time. See for, instance, Dorothy Macardle to Chief of Staff, UCDA P69/56 (7), 3 June [1924], Sinéad McCoole, *No Ordinary Women* (Dublin: O'Brien Press, 2003), 149.
5  Dorothy Macardle, Statement by Witness, NAI, BMH/457.
6  Dorothy Macardle, "Mary Comerford's Challenge to the Free State," *Éire*, 23 June 1923, 3.
7  Macardle, "Thoughts in a Hospital," *Éire*, 20 October 1923, 4–5.

Dorothy grew closer to Éamon de Valera, the president of Sinn Féin and leader of the anti-Treaty faction, in the 1920s. She accompanied him as a journalist on his tours of Munster after his release from Kilmainham in 1924. Dorothy was delighted to leave Dublin, where she felt the Free State government was gloating in its victory over the Treaty opponents, for the more congenial republican atmosphere of southwest Ireland. At train stations in Clare, de Valera was lauded by crowds "calling out wild phrases of welcome," and signs and wonders, Dorothy wrote, seemed to greet him as well. As his car approached Ennis, the previously eclipsed moon rose, "spanning the road before him like a triumphal arch." De Valera rallied the faithful by stating that republican policy remained unchanged.[8] In Cork, de Valera was "welcomed as Emmet might be if he came to Young Ireland from the dead," and enraptured crowds flocked to his orations. Dorothy concluded that the political tide had been miraculously turned in the past year: "how swiftly, amazingly, in Ireland, the harvest of sacrifice ripens!"[9]

She remained active in the Women's Prisoners Defence League over the next several years. The WPDL, co-founded by Maud Gonne MacBride and Charlotte Despard, held public meetings on Sundays to expose the plight of republican prisoners.[10] Dorothy publicized the cases of several prisoners in Northern Ireland, including Charles MacWhinney, "a Protestant [and] a disciple of Tone and Mitchel,"[11] and the future husband of her friend Linda Kearns. The prisoners, she wrote, had endured many abuses and their families suffered terribly, but they remained steadfast. One man in the Larne Camp, Patrick Nash, refused to sign an undertaking that would have released him from the camp to be with his dying mother. Mrs Nash supported his decision: "The brave woman would not ask her son to surrender. She went home and died three days afterwards, alone. The victory was Ireland's alone."[12] Dorothy reported on other northern prisoners who refused to sign undertakings, and wrote about a prisoner's death in Belfast Jail.[13]

8 Macardle, "The Rising of the Moon—to Ennis With the President," *Éire*, 23 August 1924.
9 Macardle, "In Rebel Cork," *Sinn Féin*, 20 September 1924, 1.
10 RJD, NLI MS 32,582 (42), 1 November 1922; RJD, NLI MS 32,582 (45), 31 May 1924. See also Margaret Ward, *Maud Gonne: Ireland's Joan of Arc* (London: Pandora, 1990), 135.
11 Macardle, "Republican Prisoners in the Six Counties," *Éire*, 25 October 1924, 1.
12 Ibid., 3.
13 Macardle, "Three Northern Homes," *Sinn Féin*, 25 October 1924, 2.

In the spring of 1924, Dorothy travelled to the republican strong-hold of Kerry to investigate reports of atrocities committed by Free State troops during the Civil War. Men from the IRA's Kerry brigades assisted her in locating eyewitnesses to interview, and she obtained numerous photographs "illustrating the martyrdom of Kerry."[14] Later that year, she published her findings in *Tragedies of Kerry*. One of the most notorious incidents she discovered occurred at Ballyseedy Cross, when eight republican prisoners were killed by a mine, having been ordered to the site by Free State troops. It was initially claimed that the prisoners' deaths had occurred by accident when they were sent to clear a mine obstruction, but a later inquiry led a Free State investigator to concur with the republicans that the incident was a deliberate reprisal.[15] *Tragedies of Kerry* was favourably reviewed by a republican journalist, who found it far more honest and restrained than the Great War atrocity propaganda.[16]

The writing of *Tragedies of Kerry* was not without controversy. Dorothy clashed with IRA leader Frank Aiken, who wanted the book to be a more explicit work of propaganda. Aiken told her the book was a moving tribute to the IRA men who had been killed in Kerry, but insisted she stress that Free State leaders, armed by England, bore responsibility for the atrocities in Kerry, not "poor, drunk," Free State soldiers. This would enhance the propaganda value by generating a more emotional response from readers.[17] Dorothy responded that she had tried to leave out heavy-handed, bombastic propaganda and direct indictments, but agreed to work on the book until she got it right.[18]

Dorothy published *Earth-bound*, a collection of short stories, in 1924. She had written the stories in Mountjoy and dedicated them to different friends in prison with her, such as Rosamond Jacob, Florence O'Byrne, and Nora Connolly. Many of the stories combined the political and the supernatural, two of her main interests. The title story tells of two young IRA men on the run in Wicklow during the War of Independence. They are nearly discovered by a patrol of Black

14 Dorothy Macardle to Chief of Staff, UCDA P69/56(7), 3 June [1924].
15 Dorothy Macardle, *Tragedies of Kerry* (Dublin, 1924; 14th ed., 1988), 16–19. See also Michael Hopkinson, *Green Against Green: A History of the Irish Civil War* (Dublin: Gill and Macmillan, 1988), 240–2.
16 P.B., review of *Tragedies of Kerry 1922–1923* by Dorothy Macardle, *Sinn Féin*, 19 July 1924, 5.
17 Frank Aiken to Dorothy Macardle, UCDA P69/56(8), 3 June [1924].
18 Macardle to Chief of Staff, UCDA P69/56 (6), 7 June [1924].

and Tans, but the spirit of Red Hugh O'Donal guides them to safety.[19]
During the War of Independence, Dorothy herself had trekked through
the Wicklow mountains to Glenmalure one night, accompanied by
other republican activists, and the story reflects the sense of anxiety
she must have felt, followed by relief when she arrived safely.[20] In "A
Story Without End," a republican woman named Nesta, who has
psychic powers, dreams that her husband will be executed by soldiers
dressed in green. When she tells her husband, he laughs at the notion
that an Irish army would ever execute him for treason, and at the
story's conclusion Nesta hesitantly agrees that such a situation would
never occur. However, her dream eventually comes true when Free
State soldiers execute IRA members during the Civil War. Significantly,
this story was written in Mountjoy in December 1922,[21] when Free
State soldiers carried out notorious executions of IRA prisoners.

Other stories in *Earth-bound* allude to the sacrifices made by
women in the service of Irish nationalism, and the tension between
nationalism and feminism. While Dorothy believed in fighting for
Irish independence, she drew attention to the exploitation, sacrifice,
and silencing of women in the nationalist struggle. She thought that
many nationalist men coped better with elusive ideal women and
illusions, rather than real women whom they neglected and sacrificed
in the name of nationalism. Women who embraced the ideal of silent
female suffering in the nationalist struggle were complicit in this
neglect and abuse, and undermined female solidarity, which could be
a source of empowerment. Female self-sacrifice and death, in Dorothy's
stories, were linked with the preference for ideal female figures at the
expense of real women, the idealization of fantasy worlds and death
at the expense of life in the real world, and unhealthy relationships
between mothers and daughters. When young women were not
valued and strengthened by loving mothers, and when female
solidarity was missing in their lives, their sense of self suffered, and
they became vulnerable to the appeal of self-sacrifice.[22] These insights

---

19 Dorothy Macardle, "Earth-bound," in *Earth-bound: Nine Stories of Ireland*
   (Worcester, Mass.: Harrigan Press, 1924), 7–19.
20 "Dorothy Macardle, Writer, Worker for Freedom, Dies," *Irish Press*, 24
   December 1958, 5.
21 Dorothy Macardle. "A Story Without End," in *Earth-bound*, 102–8.
22 See Jennifer Molidor, "Violence, Silence, and Sacrifice: the Mother-Daughter
   Relationship in the Short Fiction of Modern Irish Women Writers, 1890–1980"
   (PhD Dissertation, University of Notre Dame, 2007). See also Molidor, "Dying

may have come to Dorothy in prison as she reflected on her idiosyncratic journey from Dundalk to Mountjoy and Kilmainham by way of Alexandra College.

Dorothy had first turned to nationalism due to her interest in the Irish literary revival of the early twentieth century, but she critically engaged the literary conventions of the Revival by the early 1920s. "The poetry of Yeats ... *Cathleen Ní Houlihan*, the Irish Legends collected by Standish O'Grady, Lady Gregory and others, the Abbey plays and all the writings of the Celtic Twilight school" led her to Irish nationalism as a young woman.[23] She became well versed in Irish mythology and literary conventions, including feminized images of Ireland as the Sean Bhean Bhocht ("poor old woman") or as Dark Rosaleen, a beautiful young woman. Both images were heavily politicized, and were used to inspire men to fight for Ireland, but men seemed to pay little attention to the realities of women's lives which lay beyond the images. Patrick Pearse and W.B. Yeats were highly conscious of the political dimensions in their work. Pearse favoured images of passive, mournful mothers who sacrifice their sons for Ireland, reflected in poems such as "The Mother," while Dorothy preferred images of strong, assertive mothers whose love empowers their children, especially their daughters, to live rather than sacrifice themselves. The idealization of women took place in Yeats' plays and poetry as well. Men are inflamed to fight and die by iconic women, such as the symbolic "poor old woman" in his play *Cathleen Ní Houlihan*, or the beautiful Deirdre from Irish mythology, who figures in his poetry as well as his play, *Deirdre*. These symbolic women remain voiceless, and male needs are simply projected onto them.[24]

Dorothy tried to imagine and provide a voice for real women behind the ideals. In "The Portrait of Róisín Dhu," she tells the story of Nuala, a beautiful young woman from the Blasket Islands, whose portrait is painted by Hugo, a self-absorbed artist. The portrait is later mobilized for nationalist purposes. Nuala, a "Dark Rosaleen" figure, symbolizes Ireland, and some men who see the portrait are inflamed by the beauty of the ideal woman and join the struggle for

For Ireland: Violence, Silence, and Female Solidarity in the Stories of Dorothy Macardle," *New Hibernia Review*, forthcoming.

23　Dorothy Macardle, Statement by Witness, NAI BMH/457.

24　Molidor, "Violence, Silence, and Sacrifice"; Robert Welch, *The Abbey Theatre, 1899–1999* (Oxford: Oxford University Press, 1999), 15–16, 39.

Irish independence. Dorothy shows that Nuala was not merely a
beautiful icon who inspired men, but a real woman sacrificed for
nationalist ideals. She loved Hugo, who exploited and abandoned her,
and she wasted away and died. Hugo's friend Maeve was complicit in
Nuala's death, as she chose not intervene to stop the painting, and the
transformation of the real into the ideal, despite the fact that Nuala
was being idealized to death. Women, then, were sometimes complicit
in glorifying female sacrifice in the service of Irish nationalism. In
"The Portrait of Róisín Dhu," Dorothy reversed a significant Irish
literary convention found in Yeats' play *Cathleen Ní Houlihan*. In the
play, an old woman, a symbol of Ireland, inspires a young man to
fight for her, and he abandons a young woman to fight for the ideal.
His actions transform the old woman into a beautiful young woman,
symbolizing the renewal of Ireland. Yeats famously wondered if this
play had inspired men to fight for Ireland. In Dorothy's story, a real
young woman is killed in the process of being transformed into a
nationalist icon, rather than being rejuvenated. Nuala's memory
haunts Hugo, and he dies soon afterwards. Dorothy, then, questioned
and rewrote tendencies in the literature of the Irish revival which drew
on myth and seemed to value ideals and fantasies implicated in sacrifice
and death, rather than realities and life-giving human relationships
linked with female autonomy and empowerment.[25]

While in Mountjoy, Dorothy wrote a play as well as the stories in
*Earth-bound*.[26] Her play, *The Old Man*, was produced at the Abbey
Theatre in February 1925. Like *Atonement*, it dealt with "conflict
between generations leading to tragedy."[27] The historical drama's
protagonist was a young man named Robert Emmet Sheridan, who,
along with some friends, plans to rescue the Young Ireland leader
John Mitchel from prison in 1848. He is opposed by other members
of Young Ireland, as well as by his grandfather, the title character,
who then tells Young Ireland leaders Meagher and Scully that Robert
will not call off the rescue. They come to the house to talk Robert out
of the mission, and when he tries to take leave of them, he is killed by

---

25  Dorothy Macardle, "The Portrait of Róisín Dhu," in *Earth-bound*, 90–101;
    Molidor, "Mother Ireland's Daughters;" Welch, *The Abbey Theatre*, 16.
26  Rosamond Jacob recorded that "Dorothy had a great evening of writing her '48
    play," in Mountjoy. RJD, NLI MS 32,582 (43), 25 January 1923. As no script of
    this play exists, the plot has been reconstructed from reviews.
27  Cathy Leeney, "Violence on the Abbey Theatre Stage: The National Project and
    the Critic; Two Case Studies," *Modern Drama* 47:4 (Winter 2004),587.

Scully. The young idealist's death, however, is rendered meaningless when his sister announces that his friends had decided against taking part in the rescue mission.[28] Dorothy, who had been questioning the glorification of sacrifice since her imprisonment, "wished to break the convention of a politicized tragic ending by introducing a deflating element of cowardice and waste."[29] Many audience members, however, ignored the lines spoken by Robert's sister and viewed the play as straightforward political propaganda, overlooking its ambiguities. *The Old Man* was perceived as a republican allegory by many in the audience, with young Robert Emmet Sheridan standing in for radical republicans held back by cautious Free State supporters who urged moderation and compromise. For them, the tragedy lay in the grandfather losing "as much by his attempt to frustrate the effort at rescue as he would have done if it had been made and unsuccessful."[30] Several critics disliked the play due to its political nature, although they praised the acting.[31] Dorothy, who attended the opening night performance with Maud Gonne MacBride,[32] complained about actor Tony Quinn in the role of Robert Emmet Sheridan.[33]

By the late 1920s, Dorothy had developed a reputation as a working playwright. She was included in Andrew E. Malone's book *The Irish Drama*, and resented Malone for discussing her work in "the chapters on 'melodrama,' 'lesser dramatists,' and 'inferior plays'!" She also disliked the tendency of many drama critics to proclaim that politics and art were incompatible. Malone, she thought, had "fail[ed] altogether to recognize the fact that the passion for national independence can be as personal, heartfelt a thing as love or ambition … and therefore as legitimate a theme for the dramatists' art."[34] Malone's discussion of her work was not entirely negative, however. He concluded that "if Miss Macardle could free herself from the more morbid aspects of politics she would be capable of

28 Robert Hogan and Richard Burnham, *The Years of O'Casey, 1921–1926: a Documentary History* (Newark: University of Delaware Press, 1992), 265–6.
29 Leeney, "Violence on the Abbey Theatre Stage," 588.
30 Andrew E. Malone, *The Irish Drama* (New York: Charles Scribner's Sons, 1929), 269.
31 Malone, *The Irish Drama*, 269; Hogan and Burnham, 265–6.
32 Hogan and Burnham, 265.
33 RJD, NLI MS 32,582 (47), 28 February 1925.
34 Dorothy Macardle, review of *The Irish Drama* by Andrew E. Malone, *Nation*, 24 August 1929, 3; Dorothy Macardle to Frank Gallagher, Frank Gallagher Papers, NLI MS 18,340, n.d.

much finer work ... [and] something memorable will come from her pen ... her future will be watched with some anxiety by all who are on the look-out for really good Irish plays."[35]

In November 1925, Dorothy moved into a new house, creating a permanent home for the first time since her release from prison. Although her father had offered to buy her a house on Cherryfield Avenue in Ranelagh, she and Rosamond Jacob, her former cellmate at Mountjoy, moved to 16 Herbert Place. Their new house, part of a "row of smallish, light-brown brick Georgian houses with high steps" and small front gardens, overlooked the tree-lined Grand Canal, which wound through the south side of Dublin. The windows in the back rooms provided a view of the mews behind the Herbert Street houses.[36] The house was within walking distance of the center of Dublin, as well as Baggot Street, where Herbert Place residents did their shopping.[37]

Soon after Dorothy's move to Herbert Place, a number of IRA prisoners successfully escaped from Mountjoy Prison in a breakout masterminded by Dublin IRA leader George Gilmore. Although the IRA had been defeated by the Free State forces in the Civil War, the clandestine army regrouped by 1925, posing a challenge to the Free State government as it recruited and trained new members to continue the struggle for an independent republic. The IRA became visible in public demonstrations, particularly on Armistice Day, 11 November, when members battled ex-servicemen and other participants in the commemorations who carried Union Jacks and wore poppies. Following the breakout, Dorothy and Rosamond provided a safe house for a fugitive prisoner, a young man named Murphy. While staying at Herbert Place, Murphy read R. Barry O'Brien's *Dublin Castle and the Irish People* and discussed the escape, prison life, and religion with Rosamond. When guests came to visit, a wary Dorothy told Murphy to hide in another room.[38] To Dorothy's consternation, 16 Herbert Place would later serve as a safe

---

35 Andrew E. Malone, *The Irish Drama* (New York: Charles Scribner's Sons, 1929), 269.

36 Elizabeth Bowen, *Seven Winters* (New York: Alfred A. Knopf, 1962), 3, 6. Bowen was born at 15 Herbert Place in 1899.

37 Bowen, *Seven Winters*, 21.

38 RJD, NLI MS 32,582 (50), 28–29 November 1925. See also Brian Hanley, *The IRA, 1926–1936* (Dublin: Four Courts Press, 2002), 192, and Fearghal McGarry, *Frank Ryan* (Dundalk: Dundalgan Press, 2002), 5.

house for a more prominent IRA member, Frank Ryan, on several occasions.

Rosamond Jacob, Dorothy's new flatmate, was a writer and political activist who had moved to Dublin from Waterford several years earlier. The Jacobs were part of Waterford's Quaker community, and Rosamond, who was born in 1888, had been raised in a progressive, nationalist, middle-class household. In her youth, she had joined Sinn Féin, Cumann na mBan, and the Gaelic League, and spoke Irish well, unlike Dorothy, who was less interested in reviving the language.[39] A tall, thin, athletic woman with bobbed blonde hair and blue eyes, Rosamond shared Dorothy's republicanism and feminism, as well as her interests in literature, Irish history, and the occult. She contributed articles to newspapers and published several novels as well as a historical work on the United Irishmen. Dorothy and Rosamond often discussed politics and critiqued each other's writing, and their friendship provided mutual intellectual support during the 1920s and 1930s, although the two strong-willed, determined women clashed at times. They belonged to many of the same groups and had several mutual friends, such as the feminist leader Hanna Sheehy Skeffington and the journalist Frank Gallagher and his wife Cecilia. Dorothy and Rosamond both enjoyed socializing and often gave parties at Herbert Place. Frequent guests included the Gallaghers, Linda Kearns, and children's author Patricia Lynch and her husband, writer R.M. Fox. At parties, Dorothy most enjoyed playing charades, telling ghost stories, and discussing the occult.[40]

While Dorothy clearly enjoyed many close friendships, it is uncertain if she ever had any long-term, intimate relationships with men. Some men, such as the republican journalist Geoffrey Coulter, were drawn to her, but the attraction was not mutual. Coulter told Rosamond that he loved Dorothy, but when he came to visit her at Herbert Place, Rosamond felt that "Dorothy was dying to get rid of him."[41] One early

39  Damian Doyle, "Rosamond Jacob (1888–1960)," in Mary Cullen and Maria Luddy, eds, *Female Activists: Irish Women and Change 1900–1960* (Dublin: Woodfield Press, 2001), 169–79; Nadia Clare Smith, *A 'Manly Study'? Irish Women Historians, 1868–1949* (Basingstoke: Palgrave Macmillan, 2006), 138–46.
40  RJD, NLI MS 32,582 (57), 29 June 1927.
41  RJD, NLI MS 32,582 (56), 24 April 1927, 8 May 1927. Coulter, an Ulster Protestant who had been one of the few republican students at Trinity College, worked as Frank Ryan's assistant editor on *An Phoblacht* from 1929 to 1931, and then became the managing editor of the *Irish Press*. See Seán Cronin, *Frank Ryan: the Search for the Republic* (Dublin, 1980), 25.

assumption made about Dorothy was that she was "hopelessly in love with de Valera and could never look at another man."[42] Her idealization of de Valera, whom she linked with other "brilliant characters" in Irish history such as Lord Edward Fitzgerald and Wolfe Tone and John Mitchel,[43] may not, however, have taken on the dimension of romantic fantasy. Moreover, her closest relationships appear to have been with women.

Between 1926 and 1929, Dorothy lived with Florence O'Byrne, and the nature of their relationship was ambiguous. Florence, who was involved in Sinn Féin and had been imprisoned in Kilmainham during the Civil War, served as one of Dorothy's research assistants on *The Irish Republic*. They went on motoring trips around Ireland together in Dorothy's car, a Baby Austin, to conduct research and interview witnesses to events. They also crossed the border into "Carsonia," Dorothy's facetious term for Northern Ireland, in the course of their research. Dorothy had begun gathering materials for a republican-oriented history of Ireland from 1916 to 1923, and worked closely with Éamon de Valera, who, as the leader of the anti-Treaty side during the Civil War, was also interested in a history of contemporary Ireland written from a republican perspective.[44] Besides providing help with research, Florence, who was several years younger than Dorothy, moved to Herbert Place from her family's home in Rathgar, a south Dublin suburb, to attend to Dorothy as she recovered from a series of operations on her head in 1926.[45]

Dorothy and Florence's relationship soon ran into difficulties, as Dorothy tried to maintain the emotional boundaries she had so carefully constructed. She felt that Florence was overly emotional, as well as intellectually limited, and believed that the closeness Florence appeared to want would not be good for either of them.[46] Over the next few years, friends noticed increasing tensions in the relationship.

---

42  Mary Manning, "The Schoolgirls of Alexandra," *Irish Times*, 3 June 1978.
43  Dorothy Macardle to Etiennette Beuque, Terence MacSwiney Papers, UCDA P48c/71, n.d.
44  RJD, NLI MS 32,582 (49), 4 November 1925; Dorothy Macardle, Bureau of Military History Statement by Witness, NAI BMH/457. In a 1929 letter, Dorothy mentioned she had been in "Carsonia," a reference to Unionist leader Edward Carson. Dorothy Macardle to Frank Gallagher, NLI MS 18,340, n.d. [1929].
45  RJD, NLI MS 32,582 (54), 30 September 1926. O'Byrne was still a Sinn Féiner in 1933, so did not vote in the election held that year. RJD, NLI MS 32,582 (72), 28 January 1933.
46  RJD, NLI MS 32,582 (55), 19 December 1926.

Dorothy, for instance, once reduced Florence to tears in a heated argument, though they soon reconciled.[47] By 1928, she had begun to see Florence as "more a burden than an asset—partly because she is liable to morbid melancholy."[48] They permanently severed their relationship in 1933, with Dorothy pointing to Florence's "dissatisfaction with what [she] could give her in the way of attention." Rosamond Jacob thought that Dorothy could not "have cared much about Florence, and F.'s love was fairly selfish—but D. is to blame too ... just shows how utterly people misunderstand each other."[49]

There was often an undercurrent of conflict, then, when Dorothy lived with Rosamond and Florence in the late 1920s. Indeed, sexual tension came to be a pervasive part of life at 16 Herbert Place. Rosamond's relationship with the young and charismatic IRA leader Frank Ryan, whom Dorothy disliked, grew closer in late 1926, which led to further difficulties. On the night of 10 November 1926, the doorbell rang, and Rosamond, who had hoped it would be the tall, dark-haired Ryan, was disappointed to see Éamon de Valera instead. He had come to ask Dorothy, who was already in bed, if he could borrow her car, and soon left. Near midnight, Ryan, who was involved in planning demonstrations against the Armistice Day parade, came to Herbert Place with a stolen poppy for Rosamond, and stayed the night. The next morning, when Dorothy came downstairs in her dressing gown, she was shocked and furious to find Ryan in the kitchen with Rosamond. He looked at Dorothy with quizzical hazel eyes, and made his escape. Dorothy raged at Rosamond while Florence tried to calm her down.[50]

Two days later, Ryan, attempting to evade arrest for his role in disrupting "Poppy Day," came to Herbert Place again to stay the night. Dorothy, outraged again, demanded that Rosamond, "tell that young man that he was never to do it again ... it was indecent!" She was concerned that someone might complain about a man staying in their flat. Rosamond was bored with Dorothy's tantrum and thought her flatmate prudish and selfish. She asked Ryan to avoid Herbert Place for a while because of Dorothy's reaction. Ryan agreed, concerned that Dorothy would give Rosamond "a jawing."[51] The

47  RJD, NLI MS 32,582 (58), 20 June 1927.
48  RJD, NLI MS 32,582 (61), 7 December 1928.
49  RJD, NLI MS 32,582 (72), 20 February 1933, 31 March 1933.
50  RJD, NLI MS 32,582 (54), 11 November 1926.
51  RJD, NLI MS 32,582 (54), 14 November 1926.

two flatmates did not reconcile for over a week. By this time, Dorothy, feeling unwell, went to stay at Elphis, a rest home. Ryan came to Herbert Place and stayed the night once more.[52]

If Dorothy was concerned that Ryan, then twenty-four, and Rosamond, thirty-eight, would take advantage of her absence from Herbert Place to make their relationship more intimate, her concerns were baseless. This would not happen until 1929, when they "made love eagerly for nearly an hour [in the garage]" and Rosamond "could hardly believe [her] senses at first it was such a surprise ... but a motor is infernally cramped."[53] This time, neither feared that Dorothy, either in a dressing gown or other costume, would interrupt and berate them, as she and Rosamond were no longer flatmates.

Dorothy gradually became closer to Edna FitzHenry, who may have been one of her students at Alexandra. Edna worked as a writer and teacher after graduating from Trinity College, where she studied English and French.[54] She and Edna lived together for some time in the late 1920s and 1930s, first at Herbert Place and then at Creevagh, a house Dorothy bought in the south Dublin suburb of Dundrum in 1933.[55]

During the 1920s, Dorothy became intensely interested in Spiritualism and in the occult, and this lifelong fascination would later manifest itself in her novels. Spiritualism, which emerged in the nineteenth century and reached the height of its popularity in interwar Britain, held that the dead could communicate with the living. During séances, people gathered around a table and attempted to communicate with the dead through means such as table-rapping, wherein questions would be asked of spirits who were to respond by rapping the table. Spiritualism's popularity increased during the interwar period in Britain due to the massive loss of life in World War I, as traumatized survivors sought to communicate with their loved ones.[56] Dorothy (or her family members) may have attended

---

52  RJD, NLI MS 32,582 (54), 26 November 1926.
53  RJD, NLI MS 32,582 (61), 2 March 1929.
54  For Edna FitzHenry, see *Alexandra College Dublin Magazine*, vol. 7 (December 1922), 31. She was the author of a biography of Henry Joy McCracken. During World War II she taught at a school in Liverpool. See RJD, NLI MS 32,582 (96), 29 August 1941.
55  Dorothy Macardle to Owen Sheehy Skeffington, Sheehy Skeffington Papers, NLI MS 40,503(9), 27 May 1929.
56  See Jenny Hazelgrove, *Spiritualism and British Society Between the Wars* (Manchester: Manchester University Press, 2000), 14.

séances in the hopes of communicating with her younger brother, Kenneth, who had been killed during the Battle of the Somme in 1916. Kenneth himself had been interested in the paranormal, and kept a journal filled with automatic writing.[57] During the 1920s and 1930s, Spiritualism was a significant part of popular culture, and intersected with older British and Irish folk traditions about ghosts and haunted houses.[58] Reports of hauntings repeatedly appeared in popular newspapers, gaining widespread attention. Dorothy herself lived in houses she believed were haunted, and maintained, for instance, that a disruptive poltergeist frequently rearranged the furniture at Herbert Place.[59] Her first novel, *Uneasy Freehold*, depicts characters living in a haunted house in England, and Dorothy found that ghost stories could also frame stories about troubled marriages and mother-daughter relationships.

Dorothy joined the Society for Psychical Research (S.P.R.), based in London, as she was interested in extra-sensory perception as well as in ghosts. Several of her Irish friends were also interested in psychical research, such as Maud Gonne MacBride and Rosamond Jacob.[60] She soon became aware of the tension between science and Spiritualism. Even researchers in the S.P.R. were often skeptical of mediums and paranormal phenomena, and sought to carry out difficult tests to expose the frauds. Psychologists and psychiatrists also fought with Spiritualists over the interpretation of mediums and supernatural phenomena, arguing that mediums had mental disorders such as disassociation or schizophrenia, thereby undermining Spiritualist claims that mediums could experience spirit possession and communicate with the dead.[61] Dorothy was frustrated that scientists and doctors were dismissive of psychical research, because she felt research into the paranormal "should be the science of our time" and that it demanded "exact scientific method, the strictest observance of the laws of evidence, the most hard-headed investigators!"[62]

57 RJD, NLI MS 32,582 (45), 30 June 1924.
58 Hazelgrove, *Spiritualism and British Society*, 28, 175–7.
59 Ann Keating to author, 18 August 2004.
60 Margaret Ward, *Maud Gonne, Ireland's Joan of Arc* (London: Pandora Press, 1990), 106; RJD, NLI MS 32,582 (38), 13 November 1920. See also R.F. Foster, "Protestant Magic: W.B. Yeats and the Spell of Irish History," in Foster, *Paddy and Mr Punch: Connections in Irish and English History* (London: Allan Lane, 1993), for a discussion of Irish interest in occult phenomena.
61 Hazelgrove, *Spiritualism and British Society*, 121, 172–4.
62 Macardle, *Uneasy Freehold*, 257.

Her interest in psychic powers made its way into another novel, *Fantastic Summer*, in which a character much like Dorothy becomes disturbed by her ability to predict future events.

Dorothy was well provided for during the 1920s and 1930s, having an independent source of income in addition to her earnings from writing and journalism. Her father, Sir Thomas Macardle, died in December 1925. A businessman of considerable wealth, Thomas left Dorothy one-sixth of his estate. Her sister Mona, an actress in London, also received one-sixth, and her brothers John, a businessman, and Donald, a theatrical manager and actor, received two-sixths each. By the terms of their father's will, the Macardle siblings would inherit the same shares of their mother's assets when she died.[63] Dorothy could afford to travel and spend winters abroad and later bought her own house in Dundrum. After receiving her inheritance, she also repaid the money Sinn Féin had paid her for the work she had completed thus far on *The Irish Republic*, as she "realized the unsatisfactory position of a writer on a controversial issue who is an employee of a party."[64]

By the mid–1920s, Dorothy began to feel disillusioned with key figures in the Sinn Féin leadership, despite the fact that she was working steadily for the republican cause as a journalist and greatly admired Éamon de Valera.[65] In early 1925, Rosamond Jacob noted, Dorothy "dilated on the follies of [Sinn Féin] till I felt bowed under a ton weight."[66] Dorothy gradually began to move away from Sinn Féin's position regarding political abstentionism, making her receptive to her hero de Valera's new political approach. He now argued that the republican cause could most effectively be served by republican candidates entering the Dáil, or Free State Parliament, if elected, rather than boycotting the Dáil as they had the British Parliament in 1918. However, republicans strongly opposed taking the Oath of Allegiance to the Crown, which was required of deputies elected to the Dáil.

---

63  Will of Sir Thomas C. Macardle, National Archives of Ireland, d.o.g. 9 July 1926, Dublin 556. He left over thirty thousand pounds, as well as property, shares, and business holdings. Dorothy's mother died in 1933. *Irish Press*, 19 July 1933; RJD, NLI MS 32,582 (73), 25 August 1933.
64  Dorothy Macardle, Witness Statement, NAI BMH/457.
65  RJD, NLI MS 32,582 (46), 18 November 1924.
66  RJD, NLI MS 32,582 (47), 20 January 1925.

Although Dorothy was moving towards greater political pragmatism, she maintained her cherished republican ideals and belief in the nobility, selflessness, and heroism of the leaders of the 1916 Rising. These ideals led her to support the famous Abbey Theatre protest in February 1926, when she joined other republican women, such as Hanna Sheehy Skeffington and Kathleen Clarke, the widow of 1916 leader Thomas Clarke, in contesting the portrayal of the 1916 Rising in Seán O'Casey's *The Plough and the Stars*. O'Casey, one of Ireland's leading playwrights, had been aware of Dorothy for some time, and, having seen her 1922 play *Ann Kavanagh* at the Abbey, concluded that "Miss Macardle as a dramatist is nil."[67] Dorothy, the idealistic nationalist, was disturbed by O'Casey's depiction of the men of 1916. *The Plough and the Stars*, she thought, "contained a cynical disparagement of the Irish struggle. No wonder that it was more popular in London than here."[68] O'Casey, in her view, overlooked "the sincerity, the reality, the strength and depth of motive which underlay the [1916 Rising]; he substitutes for these petty vanities and sentimental cant."[69] Her participation in the protest was noted with some hostility by the *Irish Times* reviewer, who expressed a desire to "accuse her of protesting because of the failure of her play, *Ann Kavanagh*," even though the play had been popular with Abbey audiences when it was first staged.[70]

The Sinn Féin split took place following the party's Ard Fheis, or Convention, in March 1926, when Éamon de Valera formally announced his intention to form a new republican political party whose members would enter the Dáil if elected. While Dorothy supported de Valera's decision, other republicans, such as her close friend Mary MacSwiney, chose to remain in Sinn Féin and continue the policy of boycotting Free State institutions.[71] Dorothy was one of six women elected to the Fianna Fáil executive. The others were Linda Kearns, Hanna Sheehy Skeffington, Countess Markievicz, Kathleen Clarke and Margaret Pearse, the mother of the executed 1916 leader Patrick Pearse. Dorothy, to whom Fianna Fáil repre-

---

67  Hogan and Burnham, 242.
68  Dorothy Macardle, "The Fame of Irish Plays," *Irish Press*, 22 September 1931, 5.
69  Dorothy Macardle, "*Plough and Stars*, O'Casey Revival at the Abbey," *Irish Press*, 19 September 1933.
70  Hogan and Burnham, 298.
71  RJD, NLI MS 32,582 (47), 10 March 1926; Pauric Travers, *Éamon de Valera* (Dundalk: Dundalgan Press, 1994), 23–4.

sented "a miracle of resurgence"[72] was delighted to be appointed the new party's Director of Publicity, an indication of the regard in which she was held as a political propagandist.

One of Dorothy's early missions as Director was to urge friends to write letters to the editors of national and regional newspapers to contest hostile media coverage of Fianna Fáil, promote the new party's interests, and criticize the Free State government. "Cases of victimization under the Local Government Act are of special interest," Dorothy noted. "When possible please deal with the subject chosen in such a way that the note will act not only as anti-Free State propaganda but as direct propaganda for Fianna Fáil."[73] She argued with diehard republicans who opposed Fianna Fáil's approach, such as Mary MacSwiney, in personal correspondence and in the press.[74] Her rift with MacSwiney was particularly painful. When Dorothy was hospitalized for another operation on her head in June 1926, she suggested to de Valera, who was visiting her, that MacSwiney had a wax image of her and was sticking pins in it. De Valera remarked that "the occult had a great fascination for him, and he would like to study it, but he was a terrible skeptic."[75]

The 1927 elections were the first in which Fianna Fáil candidates participated, and Dorothy supported their campaigns. The successful Fianna Fáil candidates, including Éamon de Valera, entered the Dáil, despite the Oath of Allegiance which Cumann na nGaedheal refused to abolish. Between 1927 and 1932, Fianna Fáil was a minority party, and focused on challenging Cumann na nGaedheal on matters such as repressive legislation directed against republicans and other radicals. Fianna Fáil politicians still retained ties with republicans in Sinn Féin and the IRA, and sometimes defended their interests in the Dáil. Dorothy resigned from both the Directorship of Publicity and the national executive in December 1926 and August 1927 respectively, due to health reasons and misgivings over the Oath of Allegiance to the Crown that Dáil deputies were required to take.

72  Dorothy Macardle, Witness Statement, NAI BMH/457.
73  Dorothy Macardle to Hanna Sheehy Skeffington, 13 September 1926, Sheehy Skeffington Papers, NLI MS 33,606 (13).
74  See Dorothy Macardle to Mary MacSwiney, 24 April 1926, MacSwiney Papers, University College Dublin Archives [hereafter UCDA] P48a/371; MacSwiney to Macardle, 26 April 1926, UCDA P48a/371 (1); Dorothy Macardle, "Warning of Bitterness? Reply to Miss MacSwiney," *An Phoblacht*, 7 May 1926, 3.
75  RJD, NLI MS 32,582 (52), 3 June 1926.

Moreover, she did not want to be a party employee while writing *The Irish Republic*.[76]

Dorothy occasionally contributed to the *Nation*, Fianna Fáil's weekly newspaper, between 1927 and 1931. It was first edited by Seán T. O'Kelly, and then by her friend Frank Gallagher. She hoped that under Gallagher's direction the paper would become as brilliant and effective as the *Republic*, the paper edited by Erskine Childers during the Civil War.[77] The *Nation* could also be used for damage control. Dorothy's feminist misgivings about de Valera, which intensified in later years, surfaced in early 1930, when he discussed the role of Irish women during the revolutionary period in the course of an interview with a journalist from an American newspaper. He appeared to celebrate women who had remained at home while downplaying the role of republican female activists. Dorothy thought damage control was needed, because "the old charge of being anti-feminist may raise its head again any day, and the mutilated interview gives an intolerable impression."[78] A lengthier extract from the interview was soon printed in the *Nation*, highlighting de Valera's tribute to Irish women "who shared with the men all manner of dangerous work."[79]

Dorothy sought to encourage young people to submit essays for writing competitions promoted by the *Nation*. She was heartened by the contributions on the topic of "Ireland Twenty-Five Years Hence," even though only fourteen children submitted essays. She noted that most of the writers presented the Ireland of the future as an Irish-speaking sovereign republic, with a vibrant cultural scene, thriving protected industries, new technology, and emigration a thing of the past. While most upheld democratic rights, a few called for state intervention in banning foreign films and in mandating that certain clothes be worn by all citizens. The essays had a certain rehearsed quality to them, as the writers were attuned to debates in the nationalist media about cultural and economic protectionism. Dorothy

---

76 Dorothy Macardle to Honorary Secretaries, 25 December 1926, Fianna Fáil Archives, FF/A/II/1/22; Dorothy Macardle to Éamon de Valera, 29 August 1927, FF/A/II/2/26; Dorothy Macardle, Statement by Witness, NAI BMH/457; Hanley, *The IRA*, 118–25.
77 Dorothy Macardle to Frank Gallagher, 11 June 1929, Frank Gallagher Papers, NLI MS 18,340.
78 Macardle to Gallagher, 12 January [1930], Gallagher Papers, NLI MS 18,340.
79 "Heroic Irishwomen: Mr. De Valera's Tribute," *Nation*, 25 January 1930, 6.

concluded that the best essays were those in which the writers stressed their belief "that the people will remember, twenty-five years from now, the men and women who suffered to set them free."[80]

The *Irish Press*, the daily newspaper linked with Fianna Fáil, was established in 1931. Dorothy became the newspaper's drama critic. Republicans and Fianna Fáil supporters, not least of all Dorothy, had long been preoccupied with the need to establish their own popular daily paper to combat the hostile media coverage of older, more conservative dailies, such as the *Irish Times*, then favoured by ex-Unionists, and the *Irish Independent*, which was embraced by moderate nationalist supporters of the Free State.[81] Dorothy believed the late Erskine Childers had been a journalist of genius and integrity during the Civil War, when he published the *Republic*. While his newspaper had some influence, it could not compete in the arena of public opinion with the powerful established press, which treated republicans in an antagonistic manner. The outcome of the Civil War might have been different, she thought, if Childers had had a daily newspaper at his disposal to put forth the republican viewpoint.[82]

Frank Gallagher, who was close to de Valera, became the editor-in-chief of the *Irish Press*. The parameters of the *Irish Press* were largely set by Gallagher, and the paper's tone was inflected with anti-elitism, cultural nationalism, and republicanism. Gallagher wished to highlight, among other themes, independence struggles within the British Empire and news from the Irish diaspora and Catholic countries. Many of the early staff members were long-time republican activists. Several prominent women joined the staff besides Dorothy, such as Anna Kelly, who became the women's page editor.[83] The *Irish Press* was to provide Dorothy with a wider audience than the weekly *Nation* which it supplanted, and opened up a new chapter in her career as a journalist.

80  Dorothy Macardle, "Young Ireland Looks Forward: The Nation of the Future," *Nation*, 8 February 1930.
81  Mark O'Brien, *De Valera, Fianna Fáil, and the* Irish Press (Dublin: Irish Academic Press, 2001), 2–3.
82  Dorothy Macardle, "Our 'Irish' Press: Its Part in the Making of the Free State," *Nation*, 10 May 1930, 6.
83  O'Brien, 30–3.

CHAPTER FOUR

# The *Irish Press,* 1931–1936

THE EARLY 1930s marked a turning point in modern Irish political history, as the Fianna Fáil party came to power and gradually transformed Ireland into a republic. The Cumann na nGaedheal government, in the late 1920s and early 1930s, outlawed the IRA and other dissident republican organizations, and a "Red Scare" led to a crackdown on Ireland's few Communists. In 1932, the Fianna Fáil party won the election and formed a coalition government. They formed a majority government the following year, when they won an even greater number of seats in the Dáil, and remained in power until 1948. Led by Éamon de Valera, the Fianna Fáil government scaled back on repressive legislation and began the process of creating a republic through peaceful means, gradually eroding political links with Britain and "turn[ing] the Free State into a republic in all but name."[1] The state-building process led to the removal of the Oath of Allegiance, the creation of the 1937 Constitution, and the policy of neutrality during World War II. Like the Cumann na nGaedheal party, which was renamed Fine Gael in 1933, Fianna Fáil was culturally conservative, and forged close political ties with the Catholic Church, promoted the revival of the Irish language in the national schools, and maintained a strict censorship policy. While the political climate in 1932 seemed more

1 K. Theodore Hoppen, *Ireland Since 1800: Conflict and Conformity* (London: Longman, 1989), 182.

hopeful than ever to a republican like Dorothy, by the mid–1930s she clashed with more conservative members of the party on women's rights. Over the years, she found that being both a secular, liberal, feminist republican and a Fianna Fáil supporter presented considerable challenges.

Dorothy was officially the drama critic for the *Irish Press*, although she occasionally wrote on political and social issues. Her drama criticism demonstrated her deep knowledge of modern European drama and the drama of the Irish Revival. A piece on the contemporary Czech playwright Karel Capek, for instance, demonstrated her cosmopolitan appreciation for modern drama from the Continent.[2] She expressed her concern early on about changes in the staging and reception of Irish plays, and the outlook for the Abbey Theatre. After watching a performance of J.M. Synge's *The Playboy of the Western World* in the early 1930s, Dorothy commented on how the Abbey had declined since its golden age in the prewar era. The Abbey actors now performed even serious plays in an exaggerated and farcical style, and the audience laughed at nearly everything. As a serious theatregoer, Dorothy felt she had "suffered too much from the 'gigglers,' whose hyper-sensitive risibility makes them titter at the intenser moments of any play. They demolish the tragic undertones of O'Casey, even, reacting to his plays as to farce."[3]

The Gate Theatre, founded in 1928 by Micheál MacLiammóir and Hilton Edwards, became an important part of Dublin's cultural life by the 1930s. Dorothy became friendly with the Gate Theatre company, and admired the versatile MacLiammóir, who presented foreign and contemporary plays as well as the classics. She was particularly impressed by the Shakespearean productions staged at the Gate. Dorothy lauded MacLiammóir's performance in *Hamlet*, and called the sixteen-year-old Orson Welles, who played the ghost, a "very able actor."[4] She also praised the Gate's production of *Romeo and Juliet*.[5] One of Dorothy's former Alexandra students, Mary

2 Dorothy Macardle, "The Plays of Karel Capek," *Irish Press*, 29 September 1931, 5. She kept up with wider developments in drama and drama criticism by reading theatre periodicals such as *Drama*, *Theatre Arts Monthly*, and *Motley*, the in-house magazine of Dublin's Gate Theatre. See Macardle, "The Drama of To-Day: Some New Periodicals," *Irish Press*, 4 March 1932, 5.
3 Dorothy Macardle, "What is Wrong With the Abbey?" *Irish Press*, 15 September 1931, 5.
4 Dorothy Macardle, review of *Hamlet*, *Irish Press*, 3 February 1932, 4.
5 Dorothy Macardle, review of *Romeo and Juliet*, *Irish Press*, 2 November 1932, 2.

3. Advertisement for
*The Irish Republic.*
(Source: *Irish Press*,
1937)

THE FULL STORY OF
THE ANGLO-IRISH
CONFLICT

*Eamon*
**DE
VALERA**

*writes :*

"No matter what the future may hold for
the Irish nation, the seven years—1916 to
1923—must for ever remain a period of
absorbing interest. Miss Macardle's book
supplies the complete and authoritative
record. In it the story of the whole seven
years is told.

"She lived through the period, took an
active interest in affairs, was personally
acquainted with a number of the principal
actors and knew exactly where to look for
the information required."
*(From President de Valera's Preface).*

*Every Irishman MUST Read*
**THE IRISH REPUBLIC**
*by DOROTHY MACARDLE*

Manning, became associated with the Gate, which produced her first
play, *Youth's the Season-?*, in 1931. Dorothy reviewed Manning's
play, a tragicomedy satirizing a group of superficial, affluent young
adults from the south Dublin suburbs, and lauded Manning's character
development and witty dialogue, as well as the cast's acting.[6] To
Dorothy's delight, the Gate produced several plays by Anton
Chekhov, including *The Cherry Orchard* and *The Seagull*.[7] Chekhov
was one of Dorothy's favourite playwrights; she felt he "wrote for an
audience of people with more than five senses alive and awake, able
to … hear deeper and higher chords in the harmony that is woven of
man's hopes and frustrations, life's beauty and pain."[8]

6 Dorothy Macardle, review of *Youth's the Season-?* by Mary Manning, *Irish Press*,
9 December 1931, 4.
7 Dorothy Macardle, review of *The Cherry Orchard* by Anton Chekhov, *Irish Press*,
2 August 1932, 5.
8 Dorothy Macardle, "The Art of Anton Chekhov," *Irish Press*, 5 August 1932, 6.

Dorothy continued to grapple with her feelings about the relationship between nationalism and drama, and the role of the artist in national movements. After watching the Gate's production of Hendrik Ibsen's *Peer Gynt*, Dorothy noted that it satirized the Norwegian nationalist movement, particularly the nationalists' attempts to promote self-sufficiency and language restoration. This obviously resonated with the aspirations of Sinn Féin and the Gaelic League. Dorothy, who compared Ibsen to J.M. Synge, empathized with outraged Norwegian nationalists who felt "that one of the greatest of Norwegians was using his gifts to ridicule and retard his country's progress." Moreover, this situation was common in other European countries with active nationalist movements.[9]

While she admired the experimental methods of Denis Johnston's plays, Dorothy resented the treatment of Irish nationalism in *The Old Lady Says "No!"* and *The Moon in the Yellow River*. Dorothy had seen them both performed, and the plays gave her "a feeling of brainsickness ... [and] a sensation of mental vertigo." As a serious and idealistic nationalist, she objected to the anti-idealistic character of Johnston's plays and his iconoclastic portrayal of Robert Emmet and Irish nationalism. Johnston, she thought, was motivated by "bitterness against all revolutionaries" in *The Old Lady Says "No!"* Too many writers, she maintained, had constructed unrecognizable imagined Irelands, with grotesque and amoral characters.[10]

*Dark Waters*, generally acknowledged as Dorothy's best play, opened at the Gate on September 13, 1932. An *Irish Press* reviewer was especially impressed by Dorothy's dialogue and creation of suspense.[11] Hilton Edwards, Micheál MacLiammóir, and Betty Chancellor were cast in the leading roles. The play, which reflected Dorothy's lifelong interest in the supernatural, centres on Oliver Carmichael, who finds a seventeenth-century diary filled with dreams and prophesies, some of which concern his family. The audience enjoyed the play and gave Dorothy an ovation.[12] Betty Chancellor,

9  Dorothy Macardle, "Dramatists and Movements for National Freedom: The Playboy in Drama," *Irish Press*, 29 September 1932, 5. See also Macardle, review of *Peer Gynt* by Hendrik Ibsen, 28 September 1932, 3.

10  Dorothy Macardle, "Sanity, Character, and Something Else," *Irish Press*, 14 November 1932, 5.

11  "'Dark Waters,' Dorothy Macardle's Play Acclaimed at Gate," *Irish Press*, 14 September 1932.

12  "'Dark Waters,' Dorothy Macardle's Play Acclaimed at Gate," *Irish Press*, 14 September 1932, 7.

who played a character named Úna, enjoyed the role and considered *Dark Waters* "a very beautiful and moving play."[13] One audience member who sounded a more critical note, however, was Rosamond Jacob, who objected to Úna. She criticized the "conventional characterization, the sweet dewy rosebud girl with a lot of devoted chivalrous men (father, lover, and friend) all saving her from suffering, and perfectly white and un-complex romance. No psychology or subtle surprises."[14]

The cinema, by the 1930s, drew much larger crowds than the theatre, and Dorothy came to appreciate film as well as drama. Although she watched popular Hollywood movies, she preferred avant-garde foreign films with high artistic standards.[15] Dorothy admired brilliant directors, particularly those from Russia and Germany, and the early classics of world cinema. She liked the Russian directors Sergei Eisenstein and V.I. Pudovkin, and their respective films *Oktober*, *The Battleship Potemkin*, and *Storm Over Asia*, and the German directors Fritz Lang and G.W. Pabst, who directed *Metropolis* and *Kameradschaft*. She enjoyed the comedies of Charlie Chaplin and the French director René Clair. Dorothy felt that "incomparably more freely than the Expressionist Theatre, the Cinema can show us subjective emotion distorting vision, can reproduce the illusion of madness or passion, can emphasize, isolate, caricature."[16]

Dorothy appreciated Robert Flaherty's film *Man of Aran*, as she, like many Irish nationalists, idealized the Aran Islanders. In her view, they lived a simple, wholesome, noble existence in a land beyond time. The film invests mundane actions, such as fishing and breaking ground, with tremendous significance. Breaking ground for a potato patch, Dorothy wrote, "was Man breaking Nature to his will; human history since the world began." She described an exciting shark-hunting scene and the strength and skill of the shark-hunters. Those watching the film could feel proud because the Aran Islanders "are our countrymen and their actual, constant achievements are no less than these." Overall, she thought, Flaherty was a film poet, and *Man of Aran* was the ultimate counter-representation. The Irish had frequently been stereotyped as worthless drunks and violent gunmen

13  *Motley*, vol. 2, no. 6 (October 1933), 12.
14  RJD, NLI MS 32,582 (71), 13 September 1932.
15  Dorothy Macardle, "The Films of To-morrow, " *Irish Press*, 20 February 1933, 5.
16  Dorothy Macardle, "Will the Theatre Hold Its Own?," *Irish Press*, 8 September 1931, 5.

on stage, but this "faithful and beautiful motion picture" replaced the "Stage Irishman" with "that of the Man of Aran, tall and stalwart ... wielding his Herculean hammer, or beaching the curragh in which he has conquered the basking shark and weathered the ocean storm."[17]

In addition to covering theatre and cinema, Dorothy wrote on social and political issues for the *Irish Press* in the early 1930s. Her articles dealt with mothers and children in the slums, child labour, and juvenile delinquency. She highlighted the plight of poor women and their families in the North Side of Dublin.[18] She reported on the problems faced by underage newsboys who were helping to support their families. Dorothy noted the vulnerability of children who worked on the streets, some of whom turned to petty crime, and stated that some newsboys were afraid to face abusive parents if their earnings were insufficient.[19] She also wrote about children who broke the law, and expressed misgivings about sending poor children to reformatories and industrial schools. The children she observed in the Dublin Children's Court were not inherently bad, she felt, but had acted out in anti-social ways due to mischievousness and impulsiveness, as well as poverty.[20] Her interest in child welfare in Ireland and abroad was lifelong, and in the 1940s she would encounter vulnerable children on a much vaster scale.

In 1933, Dorothy co-founded the Irish Women Writers' Club with the poet Blanaid Salkeld.[21] It soon became an important source of intellectual support for Dorothy. The club's activities consisted of monthly dinners in which members read from their works in progress and discussed a variety of topics, including political and social issues. The club was open to non-fiction writers, such as historians and journalists, as well as novelists and poets. Members included

17 Dorothy Macardle, "The Man of Aran—and of Ireland," *Irish Press*, 7 May 1934, 6. See also Martin McLoone, *Irish Film: The Emergence of a Contemporary Cinema* (London, 2000), 38–44.

18 Dorothy Macardle, "Some Irish Mothers and Their Children," *Irish Press*, 14 September 1931, 6. See also Caitriona Clear, *Women of the House* (Dublin: Irish Academic Press, 2000), and Louise Ryan, *Gender, Identity, and the Irish Press: Embodying the Nation* (Lewiston, New York: Edwin Mellen Press, 2002), for other discussions of this article.

19 Dorothy Macardle, "The Newsboy as Bread-Winner," *Irish Press*, 21 September 1931.

20 Dorothy Macardle, "Children and the Law," *Irish Press*, 14 April 1932, 6.

21 Years later, she and Salkeld fought over who should get credit for starting the club. See Blanáid Salkeld to Sybil Le Brocquy, Le Brocquy Papers, NLI MS 24,232 (1), 20 July 1955.

Rosamond Jacob, Hanna Sheehy Skeffington, and the historian Mary Hayden.[22] The club was non-partisan,[23] and not all the members shared Dorothy's nationalism. Most were feminists, and the Women Writers' Club later joined other women's groups in speaking out against the 1937 Constitution. During these years, Dorothy continued to help other writers outside the Club and act as a mentor. She gave advice to a French writer, Etiennette Beuque, who was interested in Ireland and wrote a book on Terence MacSwiney.[24] She also served as a mentor to the young Maeve Brennan, who later became a celebrated short story writer and a member of the *New Yorker* staff. Maeve was the daughter of Dorothy's friends Robert and Úna Brennan. Robert, a former republican activist who had joined Fianna Fáil, worked as the general manager of the *Irish Press* and was appointed the secretary to the Irish Legation in Washington in 1933. Dorothy helped Maeve, then sixteen, with an essay published in the *Irish Press* in 1933.[25]

Dorothy's mother, Minnie Ross Macardle, died in July 1933. Although she and Minnie had never been close, she occasionally visited her mother in London. Minnie was an invalid with severe rheumatoid arthritis. In her last years, which she spent with her son Donald, she needed constant care. Minnie had always had a difficult personality, and Donald developed heart trouble from the stress of looking after his mother.[26] After Minnie's death, Dorothy began to think more about her family and how her upbringing had shaped her life. The memory of her mother and their tense relationship continued to haunt her, and found expression in her novels in the 1940s.

Her relationship with the *Irish Press* and Fianna Fáil began to change by 1935. While Dorothy continued to contribute to the newspaper, she no longer wrote regularly as the drama critic. Her friend, founding editor Frank Gallagher, formally resigned in late 1934, but stayed on until the summer of 1935, when John O'Sullivan was appointed editor. Gallagher became Radio Éireann's deputy

22  *Irish Press*, 4 February 1938, 5.
23  *Irish Press*, 16 June 1934, 5.
24  Dorothy Macardle to Etiennette Beuque, Terence MacSwiney Papers, UCDA P48c/71–4.
25  Angela Bourke, *Maeve Brennan: Homesick at the New Yorker* (London: Jonathan Cape, 2004), 113–114, 296.
26  Minnie Lucy Macardle, Death Certificate, General Register Office, Southport; RJD, NLI MS 32,582 (45), 28 March 1924.

director. Many of the *Irish Press* staffers were upset by Gallagher's treatment by the newspaper's shareholders and his resignation, and some left the paper in protest.[27]

Dorothy also began to openly question Fianna Fáil policies at this time. She especially objected to the Conditions of Employment Bill and the institutionalization of discrimination against women in industry, which feminists such as Louie Bennett and Hanna Sheehy Skeffington joined to oppose. Section 16 of the Bill, which was passed in 1936 as the Conditions of Employment Act, empowered the government to place restrictions on women's participation in various industries. During the Depression in the 1930s, male-dominated unions in Ireland and elsewhere fought to restrict women's employment to open up jobs for men. Dorothy and other feminists argued that equal pay for equal work was preferable to restrictions on the hiring of women and would protect men's jobs, as employers would refrain from hiring women over men to keep labour costs low. She maintained that social changes that had led to greater freedom and self-reliance for women were good, and that the right to work should be open to all.[28] However, she was also concerned about putting feminist principles before Fianna Fáil, as women who voted against Fianna Fáil to protest discriminatory legislation would give Fine Gael an advantage and set back the republican agenda.[29] While the Conditions of Employment Act remained on the books, Section 16 was not implemented as Ireland's small industrial sector gradually expanded.[30]

Dorothy remained outside the world of dissident republicanism that emerged following the establishment of Fianna Fáil, and which grew in strength in the mid-1930s following Fianna Fáil's formation of a majority government. While the IRA initially welcomed Fianna Fáil as an alternative to Cumann na nGaedheal, relations between Fianna Fáil and the IRA and other dissident republican organizations gradually deteriorated when Fianna Fáil came to power. Fianna Fáil's

27  Mark O'Brien, *De Valera, Fianna Fáil, and the* Irish Press (Dublin: Irish Academic Press, 2001), 65–8.
28  *Irish Press*, 13 May 1935, 8.
29  *Irish Press*, 15 June 1935, 6.
30  Catriona Beaumont, "Women and the Politics of Equality: the Irish Women's Movement, 1930–1943," in Maryann Gialanella Valiulis and Mary O'Dowd, eds, *Women and Irish History: Essays in Honour of Margaret MacCurtain* (Dublin: Wolfhound Press, 1997), 180–1.

"skilful presentation of itself as both the inheritors of the revolutionary tradition and the defenders of democracy in Ireland forced the IRA onto the defensive politically," and left it isolated and uncertain of its mission.[31] Fianna Fáil passed coercive legislation to address the threats posed by the IRA, the right-wing Blueshirts, and Communists. The IRA itself split, with left-wing members such as Peadar O'Donnell and George Gilmore leaving to form Republican Congress, which had a social rather than merely a military agenda. Cumann na mBan and Sinn Féin continued to function as republican organizations outside the Fianna Fáil fold in the 1930s, and Dorothy's old prison comrade, Mary MacSwiney, played a leading role in both groups.[32] Dorothy knew many other dissident and left-wing republicans, such as Frank Ryan, whom she had first encountered in her kitchen at Herbert Place, George Gilmore, and Peadar O'Donnell. While she shared their sympathy for the republicans in the Spanish Civil War and their opposition to the Blueshirts, a group modeled on Continental fascists, she did not share their socialist commitments and their insistence on remaining outside Fianna Fáil. Dorothy's friend Mary Manning evoked the dissident republican milieu of 1930s Dublin in *Mount Venus*, a novel in which George Gilmore appears as the character Barry McConnell, and Maud Gonne as his mother, Caroline.[33]

International events consistently assaulted Dorothy's liberal democratic principles during the 1930s. The first Fascist régime had been established in Italy in 1922, and Benito Mussolini would rule for over two decades. In 1931, Japan invaded Manchuria and committed atrocities in China. Adolf Hitler became Chancellor of Germany in 1933 and began consolidating the Nazi state. Italy invaded Abyssinia (Ethiopia) in 1935, and the League of Nations' sanctions proved ineffective. The Spanish Civil War broke out in July 1936, when right-wing nationalists led by Francisco Franco rebelled against the secular, liberal Spanish republican government. Dorothy loathed Fascism, and acknowledged, through one of her fictional characters, that "when I think of people in China, and Abyssinia, and Spain, and the Jews and the anti-Fascists, I *want* war."[34] Dorothy's hostility towards Fascism

---

31 Brian Hanley, *The IRA, 1926–1936* (Dublin: Four Courts Press, 2002), 144.
32 Fearghal McGarry, *Frank Ryan* (Dundalk: Dundalgan Press), 34–49.
33 RJD, NLI 32,582 (96), 28 August 1941; Mary Manning, *Mount Venus* (Boston: Houghton Mifflin, 1938).
34 Dorothy Macardle, *The Seed Was Kind* (Dublin: Peter Davies, 1944), 41.

was shared by many other Irish republicans in the mid-1930s. The republican newspaper *An Phoblacht*, for example, criticized the Nazi régime and condemned Italy's invasion of Abyssinia.[35]

Rather than wring her hands at the course of world events, Dorothy's response was to get more involved in international activism by the mid-1930s. She was particularly interested in the League of Nations, an assembly formed in Geneva in the aftermath of World War I. Despite her anger at Fascism, she supported the League's goal of resolving disputes diplomatically and preventing war. The League also had social sections that concentrated on humanitarian goals, and other international humanitarian groups, such as Save the Children, were headquartered in Geneva. Feminists throughout the world placed their hopes in the League of Nations as a forum to promote equal political rights for women.[36]

In September 1935, Dorothy went to Geneva to cover sessions of the League of Nations, where de Valera was presiding.[37] She was struck by the beauty and diversity of the Swiss city, marvelling at how, when walking by Lake Geneva, one could encounter people from France, Germany, India, China, the West Indies, and Africa. They were united by their belief in international cooperation, just as the many national flags hanging from different buildings "mingled fraternally by the breeze."[38] Dorothy reported on the Abyssinian crisis, which she hoped could be resolved through diplomatic means. She sympathized with the Ethiopian representative, Teele Hawariate, as he put his country's case before the League of Nations. "In Ethiopia," she wrote, "they were waiting for the white man's civilization to scatter their darkness with the thunder and lightning of guns ... too much was symbolized by those powerful [white] figures facing that small, quiet, dark-skinned man."[39] In addition to spending time with

35  Brian Hanley, *The IRA, 1926–1936* (Dublin: Four Courts Press, 2002), 174.
36  Historian Carol Miller has written extensively about women in the League of Nations. See, for instance, Carol Miller, "'Geneva – the Key to Equality': Inter-war Feminists and the League of Nations," *Women's History Review*, vol. 3, no. 2 (1994), 219–45. See also Leila Rupp, *Worlds of Women: the Making of an International Women's Movement* (Princeton: Princeton University Press, 1997), 210–22.
37  Dorothy Macardle, "The Nation's Dream of Peace," *Irish Press*, 13 September 1935, 6; "[Mr. De Valera's Speech at Geneva], Deep Effect on Listeners," *Irish Press*, 17 September 1935, 2.
38  Dorothy Macardle, "The Nations' Dream of Peace," *Irish Press*, 13 September 1935, 6.
39  Dorothy Macardle, "The Crisis and the Covenant," *Irish Press*, 25 September

de Valera and the Irish representatives, Dorothy liaised with feminists and children's advocates in Geneva, and wrote about the concerns brought by feminists to the League of Nations. An international body like the League of Nations, she believed, could redress injustices such as unequal nationality laws for women and men. She returned to Dublin pleased with what she had seen in Geneva.[40]

When Dorothy saw the newspaper on 20 February 1936, she was surely as horrified as anyone else in Dublin. A nineteen-year-old man named Edward Ball had been questioned by the police about the murder of his mother, Vera, whose bloodstained car, a Baby Austin like Dorothy's, had been found in Booterstown, a south Dublin suburb.[41] Although "the crime of mother murder was extremely rare in Ireland," it seemed to have occurred in Booterstown,[42] and Edward Ball was charged with murdering his mother.[43] Dorothy knew of Edward, as he was interested in theatre and occasionally landed small roles in various productions at the Gate Theatre, where he became romantically involved with stage manager Cecil Monson. Edward came from an affluent but dysfunctional Dublin family and had an English public school education at Shrewsbury. His parents had separated in his childhood, and he lived with his erratic, temperamental mother. His father, Dr Charles Preston Ball, a nerve specialist, lived elsewhere in Dublin. On the night of 18 February Edward killed his mother with a hatchet, and disposed of the corpse in the Irish Sea. It was never recovered. At his trial in May 1936, a jury found Edward guilty but insane, and he was committed to the Central Criminal Lunatic Asylum in Dundrum, a short distance from Dorothy's house, Creevagh. She and many of the people associated with the Gate were sympathetic towards Edward, and she visited him in the asylum.[44] In

1935; Dorothy Macardle, "A Journalist in Geneva," *Alexandra College Dublin Magazine*, vol. 8 (December 1938), 3–6.

40  Dorothy Macardle, "Women's Meeting at Geneva," *Irish Press*, 18 September 1935, 8; "The Legal Status of Women," *Irish Press*, 19 September 1935, 1; "Women's Cause at Geneva," *Irish Press*, 30 September 1935, 6; RJD, NLI MS 32,582 (78), 3 January 1936. See also Michael Kennedy, *Ireland and the League of Nations* (Dublin: Irish Academic Press, 1996).

41  *Irish Press*, 20 February 1936, 1.

42  *Irish Press*, 19 May 1936, 9.

43  *Irish Press*, 22 February 1936, 1.

44  *Irish Press*, 25 May 1936. For more on the Ball case, see Kenneth Deale, *Memorable Irish Trials* (London: Constable, 1960); Richard Cobb, *A Classical Education* (London: Chatto and Windus, 1985); Kieran Fagan, "Unnatural Born Killer," *Irish Times*, 13 December 1994, 13.

the time they spent together, Dorothy came to care for Edward. He was released in the late 1940s, partly due to her intervention. Dorothy later creatively reimagined the Ball case in one of her novels.

The mid-1930s marked a new beginning for Dorothy, as she began to take on a more critical role within Fianna Fáil and the Irish Free State while retaining close ties to power. She made known her objections to the Conditions of Employment Bill, which foreshadowed her open opposition, again based on feminist principles, to the 1937 Constitution backed by Fianna Fáil. At the same time, her belief in liberal internationalism was reinforced by her experience at the League of Nations, which anticipated the humanitarian impulse that led her to work with European refugees during and after World War II, and to write *Children of Europe*.

CHAPTER FIVE

# *The Irish Republic* and An American Tour, 1937–1939

DOROTHY MACARDLE ACHIEVED fame as a historian with the publication of *The Irish Republic* in 1937. Her popular political history of Ireland from 1916 to 1923 constructed and transmitted a coherent and influential republican interpretation of the Irish revolution to a wide audience, and was pressed into service for its political usefulness by Éamon de Valera and the Fianna Fáil party from the 1930s to the 1960s. Although she produced a celebrated nationalist work that made her famous in Ireland, much had changed during the decade in which she wrote the book, and by the late 1930s she fell out with Fianna Fáil and became more interested in world events.

*The Irish Republic* may be located within the "history wars" that raged in Ireland in the 1920s and 1930s. During the 1920s, the Free State, pro-Treaty partisans then in power clearly had the upper hand in these propaganda battles. With skilled polemicists and a sympathetic media, they were in a prime position to put forth their view of the Anglo-Irish Treaty and the Civil War, to the detriment of the republican faction. This began to change in the 1930s when Fianna Fáil was in power. Frank Pakenham's *Peace By Ordeal*, published in 1935, interpreted the 1921 Anglo-Irish Treaty negotiations in a manner more favourable to de Valera and the opponents of the Treaty.[1]

1 Patrick Murray, "Obsessive Historian: Éamon de Valera and the Policing of His

Éamon de Valera was the prime mover in the making of *The Irish Republic*. While mapping out a strategy for reentering politics in the aftermath of the Civil War, he longed for a documents-based history of revolutionary Ireland that situated him at the centre of the narrative, validated the republican perspective, and effectively counteracted the opposition. He had originally approached his secretary, Kathleen O'Connell, who collected his papers as well as other relevant documents, but the demands on her time were such that she could not write the book.[2] He then turned to Dorothy, who was thinking along similar lines in the 1920s and had collected material for a history of Irish republicanism since 1916.[3] As a republican journalist, she had much experience in refuting hostile anti-republican polemics and propaganda. In addition, de Valera may have felt that Dorothy would be a more credible historian as she had not been raised in the republican tradition.[4] The shape and scope of *The Irish Republic* largely conformed to that outlined by de Valera in the 1920s, as he closely supervised the writing process.[5]

Dorothy believed in promoting the republican view of contemporary history to the wider public to counteract British and pro-Treaty historical narratives which vilified republicans. The republicans, in her view, were not only the underdogs in the revolution, but in historiography and in the media as well. "Journalists and fiction writers and ... historians more or less hostile to Ireland," she maintained, had "present[ed] a ... somewhat incredible picture in which a small band of terrorists domineers over the Irish populace and holds the British Empire at bay." The time had come for "an account of the Irish Republican struggle from the viewpoint of an Irish Republican."[6]

Reputation," *Proceedings of the Royal Irish Academy*, Vol. 101c, 37–65 (2001), 57–8.

2 Eunan O'Halpin, "Historical Revisit: Dorothy Macardle, *The Irish Republic* (1937)," *Irish Historical Studies*, vol. 31, no. 123 (May 1999), 390; Murray, 59–60.

3 Dorothy Macardle, Statement by Witness, NAI BMH/457.

4 Dorothy noted in her foreword to *The Irish Republic* that although she was "Anglo-Irish by parentage and with the Allies during the world war in sympathies," she was convinced that "the principles of justice and democracy seem to rest on the Irish side" in Ireland's conflict with Britain. Dorothy Macardle, *The Irish Republic* (London: Victor Gollancz, 1937; 4th ed., Dublin: Irish Press, 1951), 23. All references are to the 1951 edition.

5 Murray, 60–1.

6 Macardle, 23.

4. Dorothy Macardle with the Irish Women Writers' Club, 1938.
(Source: *Irish Press*, 1938)

Despite Dorothy's insistence that de Valera left her alone to write her history as she saw fit, the evidence points to a considerable amount of intervention on de Valera's part. Over the years, he visited Dorothy at home on a number of occasions to discuss the book.[7] She resented de Valera's interference in regard to her hard-hitting treatment of repressive legislation under the Cosgrave government. In 1935, de Valera wanted her to change the book "to suit his altered ideas of what [should] be said about the crimes of the Cosgrave government in the past – all is to be watered down now, & no 'bitter' truth told."[8] By the mid-1930s, the Fianna Fáil government had itself implemented, in response to threats posed by the IRA and the Blueshirts, the repressive legislation that republicans had found objectionable under the Cosgrave government.

7 For Rosamond Jacob's help with newspaper research at the National Library of Ireland, see RJD, NLI MS 32,582 (48), 23 June 1925, 31 July 1925. For her comments on de Valera's discussions with Macardle, see RJD, NLI MS 32,582(48), 21 June 1925, 26 June 1925.
8 RJD, NLI MS 32,582 (77), 25 August 1935.

*The Irish Republic* began with an overview of nineteenth-century Ireland, and went on to examine the 1916 Rising, the War of Independence (1919–21), and the Civil War (1922–3) from a republican perspective. Dorothy established the republican tradition with the 1798 Rising, and traced this tradition through to the early twentieth century. The Irish Republican Brotherhood (IRB) inherited the revolutionary tradition, which coexisted with constitutional politics during the nineteenth and twentieth centuries. Dorothy emphasized the democratic and nonsectarian dimension of Irish republicanism, as well as the role of Protestants in the nationalist movement.[9]

Dorothy worried about democracy during the 1930s, and sought to demonstrate the democratic nature of Irish republicanism. She stressed that Sinn Féin had won the 1918 elections, and therefore had a popular mandate for its actions during the War of Independence. Republican candidates for the Dáil had also been successful in the May 1921 elections, again confirming widespread republican and anti-Partitionist sentiment among the Irish electorate.[10] Irish representatives had tried to gain admittance to the Paris Peace Conference in 1919, demonstrating their commitment to resolving conflicts through diplomacy, but did not gain a hearing, underscoring the limitations of Woodrow Wilson's rhetoric about freedom for small nations.[11] The British government, the Unionists, and the Irish Free State supporters were undemocratic, Dorothy argued, in contrast to the Irish republicans. While the republicans addressed British security concerns and suggested guarantees by the British Commonwealth of Nations, Britain threatened to renew the war if the 1921 Treaty, which allowed for dominion status rather than independence, was not accepted.[12] The Republicans upheld the elected Dáil, which the Free State supporters destroyed.[13] Overall, then, Dorothy was keen to marshal arguments emphasizing the democratic credentials of the republicans and the antidemocratic nature of their opponents.

The account of the Civil War in *The Irish Republic* provoked more controversy in Ireland than the account of the War of Independence,

9 Macardle, 36–50.
10 Macardle, 265–7, 453–5.
11 Macardle, 297–8.
12 Macardle, 544–8.
13 Macardle, 809.

since it was the Civil War rather than the earlier conflict that shaped Irish party politics from the 1920s onwards. The two main parties, Fine Gael and Fianna Fáil, traced their origins to the early post-Civil War period. Fine Gael supporters had accepted the 1921 Anglo-Irish Treaty, while Fianna Fáil was founded in 1926 by anti-Treaty republicans who chose to enter the Dáil and advance their republican agenda through political means. In Dorothy's narrative, instances of Free State violence, such as the executions of republican prisoners and the Ballyseedy Cross incident,[14] received much attention, while republican violence was downplayed. The republicans, particularly de Valera, were presented as deeply principled, doing their utmost to prevent conflict until driven to fight by the provocations of the Free Staters, and, subsequently, trying to find a peaceful resolution to the Civil War.[15] When the IRA called a ceasefire in the spring of 1923, Dorothy maintained, the victory belonged to Britain, not Ireland.[16] The partition of the island into the Irish Free State and Northern Ireland remained permanent after the failure of the Boundary Commission, in 1925, to renegotiate the border.[17]

The book concluded on an optimistic note. A decade after the disillusionment of the Boundary Commission, Dorothy wrote, Ireland was in a far stronger position than that which prevailed under William Cosgrave's Free State government in the 1920s. The individual responsible for this transformation was Dorothy's political hero, Éamon de Valera, now the Taoiseach, or Prime Minister. She listed some of his steps towards the creation of a republic, all of which had been achieved through political means since Fianna Fáil came to power in 1932. A major achievement was the termination of the Oath of Allegiance to the British Crown, which paved the way for greater Irish sovereignty.[18] At the same time, Dorothy argued, British political thought was becoming more progressive. The present generation, she hoped, "may make anew the opportunity that, in 1921, was so tragically wasted, and may see an Irish Republic make, with the British Commonwealth of Nations, a compact of amity and peace."[19]

14  Macardle, 822, 839–40.
15  Macardle, 748–50, 776.
16  Macardle, 857–61.
17  Macardle, 887.
18  Macardle, 897.
19  Macardle, 897.

*The Irish Republic* is of lasting historical significance. Emerging at a time when Éamon de Valera was consolidating his vision of an independent Ireland, it became a foundational text of the republic, transforming a marginal, alternative republican history into an orthodox, state-sanctioned national narrative that would be criticized by later historians. At the time, the book was widely reviewed in Irish newspapers and journals, and was also noticed in Britain, where it was first published by Victor Gollancz. A laudatory review appeared in the Fianna Fáil newspaper, the *Irish Press*, in March 1937. The reviewer complimented Dorothy's narrative style and ability to tell a captivating story, while simultaneously presenting a detailed analysis in a rigorous fashion. She was commended for her strategy of citing British and other non-republican sources, which supported her case far more convincingly than a complete reliance on partisan republican sources.[20] While the reviewer held republican sympathies and admired de Valera, "E.A." also pointed out omissions and elisions reflective of Dorothy's own partisanship. Dorothy discussed the Civil War "without mentioning some of the worst acts of Republicans … [she] is overkind in dealing with republican excesses."[21] To support this contention, "E.A." posited that if Free State troops rather than republicans had been responsible for the death of Free State Deputy Seán McGarry's child, Dorothy would have treated the matter differently. She had simply mentioned that when the IRA burned Free State politicians' homes during the Civil War to avenge the execution of republicans, "a child was accidentally injured and afterwards died."[22] On the whole, however, "E.A." believed *The Irish Republic* to be an admirably well-researched, engaging, accurate, and thorough account of contemporary Irish history.

A sarcastic review appeared in the *Irish Independent*, a paper favoured by Fine Gael supporters. During the Civil War, their sympathies had been with the Free State forces, collectively presented in a negative light in *The Irish Republic*. The *Irish Independent* reviewer, who was anti-republican and hostile to de Valera, doubted that *The Irish Republic* was truly a work of history. "If only," the reviewer

20  "E.A.," review of *The Irish Republic* by Dorothy Macardle, *Irish Press*, 17 March 1937, 8.
21  "E.A.," review of *The Irish Republic* by Dorothy Macardle, *Irish Press*, 24 March 1937, 8.
22  Ibid., 11; Macardle, *The Irish Republic*, 824.

lamented, "Miss Macardle's view-point was not so constantly forced upon with Mr. de Valera's infallibility ... not even proclaimed but taken for granted." The reviewer referred to various transgressions by the IRA before and after the outbreak of the Civil War in June 1922. Implying that Dorothy was a hero-worshipper, the writer noted that "the book closes fittingly with a gushing tribute to 'the quiet tenacity of de Valera's leadership.'"[23]

In the British press, a positive review of *The Irish Republic*, written by W.R. LeFanu, appeared in the *Times Literary Supplement*. Thus, British readers interested in contemporary events were aware of Dorothy's book, as the *TLS* review dovetailed with the publicity given *The Irish Republic* by the Left Book Club, which was founded by Victor Gollancz. LeFanu praised Dorothy's illuminating analysis of the different political actors at the time of the 1916 Rising. He noted that she downplayed military history and detailed accounts of IRA strategies and campaigns due to "her apparent intention to show the Republic as a constitutional democratic government working with success in abnormal conditions."[24]

The Irish Women Writers' Club honoured Dorothy at their Fourth Annual Banquet, held at the Gresham Hotel in Dublin on 3 February 1938. She spoke about how she had driven around Ireland conducting hundreds of interviews with people who had lived through the revolutionary years, and she had struggled with shaping the mass of oral and written material into a coherent whole. Writing a massive work of contemporary history kept her from doing what she most enjoyed, writing plays and traveling.[25] Rosamond Jacob, a club member whose new book, *The Rise of the United Irishmen*, was also being honoured that evening, noted that Dorothy seemed to be enjoy-

---

23 Review of *The Irish Republic* by Dorothy Macardle, *Irish Independent*, 15 March 1937. Other reviews appeared in *Ireland To-day*, a progressive journal that lasted only two years, and the conservative *Catholic Bulletin*. There was no review in the leading American newspaper, the *New York Times*, until the publication of an American edition of *The Irish Republic* in 1965.

24 W.R. LeFanu, review of *The Irish Republic* by Dorothy Macardle, *Times Literary Supplement*, 24 April 1937, 306. Dorothy was asked to give a speech on *The Irish Republic* to the Left Book Club in 1937. Dorothy Macardle to Owen Sheehy Skeffington, Sheehy Skeffington Papers, NLI MS 40,505(5), 8 December 1937. For more on the Left Book Club and its impact, see Stuart Samuels, "The Left Book Club," *Journal of Contemporary History*, vol. 1, no. 2 (April 1966), 65–87.

25 "Women Writers' Club Banquet, Dorothy Macardle Honoured," *Irish Press*, 4 February 1938.

ing the recognition.[26] A letter of appreciation from Éamon de Valera was read to the gathering, as he was unable to attend. In addition to Jacob, Dorothy's friends attending the dinner included Linda Kearns, Edna FitzHenry, Maud Gonne MacBride, Patricia Lynch and her husband R.M. Fox, Florence O'Byrne, and Máire Comerford, a republican activist who now contributed to the *Irish Press*.

Dorothy occupied an uncertain position in the Irish historical profession at a time when major innovations were taking place in the discipline. A non-academic historian with a degree in English, she read widely in Irish history and wrote plays with historical settings. *Ann Kavanagh* took place during the 1798 Rising, while *The Old Man* was set in 1848, when another rebellion broke out. Her only experience teaching Irish history was in Kilmainham Gaol, where she offered "Revolutionist Irish History" to fellow prisoners. In the late 1930s, when *The Irish Republic* was published, a modern university-based historical profession was emerging in Ireland. Its leading figures, R.D. Edwards of University College Dublin and T.W. Moody of Trinity College, founded the professional journal, *Irish Historical Studies*, in 1938. The journal did not deal with contemporary history, which it defined as events that had taken place within the preceding fifty years. Thus, journalists, non-academic historians, and university historians of an older school, rather than the new professionals, tended to write contemporary history. Academic historians were aware of *The Irish Republic*, however, and R.D. Edwards wrote that "Miss Macardle has performed a very great service for her subject."[27]

Dorothy could be located in the Irish tradition of the journalist-historian involved in politics, as well as in the tradition of Irish nationalist women historians. As a historian, she resembled Alice Stopford Green, a Free State senator and historian of an older generation, and her contemporaries Helena Concannon, a Fianna Fáil senator as well as a historian, and the politically active Rosamond Jacob, who wrote on eighteenth-century Irish history.[28] Dorothy was helped by other women historians and researchers, such as Rosamond Jacob and Mary Hayden, who taught history at UCD. Her research

26  RJD, NLI MS 32,582(83), 3 February 1938.
27  R.D. Edwards Papers, UCDA [University College Dublin Archives], LA22/1135 (7).
28  For more on these historians, see Nadia Clare Smith, *A 'Manly Study'? Irish Women Historians, 1868–1949* (Basingstoke: Palgrave Macmillan, 2006).

assistants included Florence O'Byrne and Fiona Connolly. While eminent male historians had often turned history into a family industry in which their wives and children helped with research and writing, Dorothy had a network of women friends who helped her. Dorothy's attainment of state recognition for her work, and her close ties to the government, contradict the truism that historians who gain access to state power tend to be *male* writers of political histories that bolster state power.[29] In a wider European perspective, Dorothy compares with the politically committed women historians in states with strongly nationalist régimes who wrote contemporary history. Women may have been drawn to contemporary history because it was a new subfield, lacking in academic prestige and less likely to be guarded by intellectual gatekeepers in the academy.[30]

Although *The Irish Republic* brought Dorothy state recognition upon its publication in 1937, that year marked a turning point in her attitude to Éamon de Valera and Fianna Fáil. Dorothy openly expressed her opposition to one of de Valera's projects, the 1937 Constitution, which angered her more than the Conditions of Employment Bill she had criticized in 1935. She and other Irish feminists were particularly concerned about Article 41, which declared that "the State recognizes that by her life within the home, woman gives to the state a support without which the common good cannot be achieved ... the State shall, therefore, endeavour to ensure that mothers shall not be obliged by economic necessity to engage in labour to the neglect of their duties in the home."[31] Women activists believed that this article in the Constitution, following on the heels of the Conditions of Employment Act, could be used by the government to further restrict women's employment. Some felt the article rang hollow, as the social legislation in place was insufficient to allow poor mothers to remain at home, rather than take on gruelling, low-wage jobs. There was little subsidized housing in the 1930s, no national health insurance, and no family allowances.

29  Bonnie Smith, *The Gender of History: Men, Women, and Historical Practice* (Cambridge, Mass.: Harvard University Press, 1998), 1, 3, 7–8, 11.
30  I am indebted to Ilaria Porciani for discussing this point with me.
31  Catriona Beaumont, "Women and the Politics of Equality: the Irish Women's Movement, 1930–1943," in Maryann Gialanella Valiulis and Mary O'Dowd, eds, *Women and Irish History: Essays in Honour of Margaret MacCurtain* (Dublin: Wolfhound Press, 1997), 181–4.

Women's organizations, including the Irish Women Writers' Club, spoke out strongly against the Constitution's clauses regarding women, writing letters to the press and sending delegations to meet with de Valera. In May 1937, Dorothy, the vice-chair of the National Council of Women's Standing Committee on Legislation Affecting Women, wrote to the *Irish Press* on women's concerns regarding the Constitution.[32] In addition, she sent de Valera a private letter, suggesting ways to compromise on the Constitution. "As the Constitution stands," Dorothy told him, "I do not see how anyone holding advanced views on the rights of women can support it, and that is a tragic dilemma for those who have been loyal and ardent workers in the national cause."[33] The National Council of Women communicated with the International Council of Women about the Constitution, and representatives from international women's groups wrote to de Valera to express concern. Miss Archdale of the Six Point Group mentioned the "invaluable support" given by Irish delegates to women's groups at the League of Nations. She then pointed out that if Irish women had remained at home, in keeping with the spirit of the Constitution, "Ireland's fight for freedom would not have been so successful." As a lifelong freedom fighter, de Valera could "surely not wish to deprive Irish women of the freedom for which they have also fought."[34] Dorothy, as an Irish feminist in contact with international feminists she had met in Geneva, helped draw attention to Irish women's concerns about the Constitution and mobilize an international lobbying effort.

The Constitution was ratified, but the women activists managed to have some of the more controversial language amended. Dorothy soon became involved in the WSPL (the Women's Social and Political League, later renamed the Women's Social and Progressive League), which was formed in late 1937 in response to the controversy surrounding the Constitution. The WSPL's agenda included supporting women candidates for election to the Dáil and acting as a pressure group monitoring legislation of interest to women. The WSPL sponsored lectures on social issues, inviting prominent public speakers. The organization helped form a link between the feminist movements

32 See NAI D/T s9880 for women's letters regarding the Constitution. See also Dorothy Macardle, letter to the *Irish Press*, 17 May 1937.
33 Macardle to de Valera, NAI D/T s9880, 21 May 1937.
34 Betty Archdale to Éamon de Valera, NAI D/T s9880, 14 June 1937.

of the early and late twentieth centuries during the 1930s and 1940s, a time when feminism seemed dormant.[35]

Dorothy journeyed to Geneva again in August 1937, revealing her continuing commitment to internationalism and the League of Nations' mission. She attended a conference and lectures on international relations, met with members of League of Nations societies from many different countries, and took part in lively political discussions.[36] Her experience in Geneva became the basis for her novel *The Seed Was Kind*, which begins with the characters meeting at the League of Nations for a summer school program for students in 1937. Later that year, Dorothy joined the Council of the Institute for the Study of International Affairs in Dublin.[37] Now that she had completed *The Irish Republic*, she decided that her next book would be a history of the League of Nations' humanitarian work, and spent the early summer of 1938 conducting research in Switzerland and France. She secured a valuable interview in Paris with Malcolm Davis, the European Director of the Carnegie Endowment for International Peace.[38] By August, however, this plan had fallen through. The British League of Nations Society, upon hearing she intended to write on the League's humanitarianism, announced that they intended to write a book on the topic.[39]

The latter months of 1938 were inauspicious for Dorothy, as she was in England at the time of the Munich Crisis, when the fear of war was widespread. It felt like "London might be wiped out any day … gas-masks, newspaper scares, incessant wondering as to what was likely to happen."[40] In late September 1938, the Munich con-

---

35 RJD, NLI MS 32,582 (83), 24 November 1937. See also Catriona Beaumont, "Women and the Politics of Equality: the Irish Women's Movement, 1930–1943," in Maryann Gialanella Valiulis and Mary O'Dowd, eds., *Women and Irish History: Essays in Honour of Margaret MacCurtain* (Dublin: Wolfhound Press, 1997), 173–88.

36 Dorothy Macardle to Owen Sheehy Skeffington, Sheehy Skeffington Papers, NLI MS 40,505(5), 8 December 1937. For the Irish League of Nations Society, founded in 1923, see the Le Brocquy Papers, NLI MS 24,243 and NLI MS 23,240.

37 "Ireland and World Politics, New Study Group Formed," *Irish Press*, 30 October 1937, 4.

38 Dorothy Macardle to Malcolm Davis, CEIP [Carnegie Endowment for International Peace], Centre European Records File 168.9, Columbia University Rare Books and Manuscripts, 25 June 1938.

39 RJD, NLI MS 32,582 (85), 11 August 1938, 25 August 1938.

40 Dorothy Macardle to Kathleen O'Connell, UCDA P155/127, 24 October [1938].

ference concluded with Adolf Hitler being granted the Sudetenland, an area of Czechoslovakia with many German speakers, in the belief that this would satisfy his territorial demands. The Munich Crisis marked the high point of the appeasement policy towards Hitler, who invaded Czechoslovakia in March 1939. Dorothy strongly opposed the appeasement of the Nazis, and felt "rage and misery over the treatment of the Czechs." She had long admired Czechoslovakia, which she viewed as a liberal, tolerant, cultured democracy.[41] Britain, she thought, could "never pose as the champion of little nations again" after its role in dismembering Czechoslovakia. She wanted to go to Prague to do relief work immediately, but was prevented by illness.[42]

In the spring of 1939, a few months after her fiftieth birthday, Dorothy travelled to the United States for a lecture tour. The Irish government sent her to lecture on Irish literature at the New York World's Fair, where Ireland had a pavilion. She shared both her knowledge of Irish literature and her internationalist humanitarian views with American audiences. The lecture tour was part of a public relations initiative by the Department of the Taoiseach to promote awareness of Ireland and its culture to American audiences. According to the plan, Dorothy, UCD Celtic Studies scholar Eoin MacNeill, and folklorist Séamus Delargy would deliver lectures in New York, Boston, and Chicago.[43]

The New York World's Fair opened on April 30, 1939, and was a great spectacle. There were fireworks, musical and dance performances, speeches, and amusements. Officials from different nations created pavilions with exhibits on their country's history, culture, and trade. Ireland's shamrock-shaped pavilion, designed by Dublin architect Michael Scott, featured exhibits on the history of Ireland and the Irish contribution to the United States, a stained glass panel of "the four green fields of Erin," by Evie Hone, paintings, sculptures, handicrafts, and Irish exports. The pavilion was officially dedicated by the Táiniste (Deputy Prime Minister) Seán T. O'Kelly, as Éamon de Valera could not come. The dedication ceremony was attended by the mayor of New York, Fiorello La Guardia, who called the Irish

---

41 Macardle to O'Connell, UCDA P155/127, 24 October [1938]; Dorothy Macardle, *The Seed Was Kind* (London: Peter Davies, 1944).
42 Dorothy Macardle to Kathleen O'Connell, UCDA P155/127, 24 October 1938, 25 November 1938.
43 NAI, D/TAOIS s9215A.

pavilion "a shrine to those people still striving for freedom," and Dorothy's friend Robert Brennan, the Irish Minister to Washington. Besides lecturing at the World's Fair, Dorothy visited other countries' pavilions and the League of Nations' Pavilion, and probably attended the World Congress of Writers held there.[44]

The World Congress of Writers brought together about one thousand writers who shared Dorothy's views on the role of writers in a world on the brink of war. They were concerned about attacks on the freedom of the press, and free expression, which had been restricted or eliminated in Fascist and Communist countries. Dorothy was involved in the Irish branch of the International P.E.N. Club,[45] an organization whose acronym stood for poets, playwrights, essayists, editors, and novelists, which defended the rights of writers around the world. At the World's Fair in May 1939, the American branch of P.E.N. sponsored a dinner in which participants listened to speeches and resolved to use "every effective means to reach the consciences of those who live behind the barriers of the regimes of force and to reawaken in them the notion of human ideals." The president of the American P.E.N. branch was another journalist named Dorothy. Dorothy Thompson, a celebrated columnist with the *New York Herald Tribune* as well as the wife of novelist Sinclair Lewis, was one of America's most outspoken anti-Fascist journalists. The charismatic Thompson, who had begun her career as a journalist in Europe in the 1920s, called for "a conspiracy of poets to offset the innumerable [other] conspiracies that have made this world a nightmare."[46]

Mills College, a women's college in California, invited Dorothy to give the commencement speech the following month. She left New York, where she gave a broadcast, and visited Boston and Washington, D.C. to give lectures and visit friends before heading to California. Mary Manning Howe lived with her husband in Boston, which had a significant Irish-American community. The city was also the home of

---

44 "Ireland Expresses Pride in Fair Role as Twin Exhibits Are Dedicated in the Rain," *New York Times*, 14 May 1939, 40; "Role of News in Recording World History Discussed at Writer's Congress," *New York Times*, 11 May 1939, 23.

45 "P.E.N. Club Meeting, Influence of Nationality on Literature," *Irish Press*, 5 February 1935.

46 "Role of News in Recording World History Discussed at Writer's Congress," *New York Times*, 11 May 1939, 23; Peter Kurth, *American Cassandra: The Life of Dorothy Thompson* (Boston: Little, Brown, and Company, 1990), 307–8.

Dorothy's friend Helen Landreth, a librarian at Boston College who had visited Ireland earlier in the decade and who wrote on Irish history. Landreth later wrote a biography of their mutual friend Mary Childers, Erskine Childers' widow, who was originally from Boston. In Washington, D.C., Dorothy gave a lecture to the Women Journalists' Club and may have visited her friend Robert Brennan, the Irish Minister to Washington, and his family. On her cross-country journey to the West Coast, she imagined she saw pioneers, Indians, and gold miners when she looked out the train window at the unfamiliar landscape. She was struck by the High Sierras and the train's descent into San Francisco, when the early morning fog gave way to blazing sunshine, so different from home. California, she decided, must be "where good Dubliners go when they die." She explored San Francisco, where she spoke on Ireland at the Golden Gate Exposition and addressed the English-Speaking Union, and then went to Oakland, where Mills College was located.[47]

Mills College, founded in the nineteenth century as the first Protestant college for women on the West Coast, greatly appealed to Dorothy. Modeled on Eastern women's colleges such as Wellesley and Mount Holyoke in Massachusetts, Mills had expanded and modernized since the 1920s under the guidance of its president, Aurelia Reinhardt. Dorothy stayed at Mills as a guest of Reinhardt, a language and literature scholar as well as an administrator. Mills reminded Dorothy of Alexandra, as both colleges encouraged social and political engagement as well as academics. The college sponsored lectures and seminars on world events, so a commencement speaker associated with the League of Nations was especially welcome. As she toured the campus, admiring the gardens and Mission-style buildings, she noticed the music building, and the art gallery, and the theatre, a pleasing sight for a playwright like herself. She met with Mills students and felt "young for a day," refreshed by the idealism and optimism of the young women about to graduate.[48]

Her commencement speech was on "The Common Enemy." The enemy, Dorothy declared, was "the host composed of ignorance,

---

47  Dorothy Macardle File, BBC Written Archives Centre [hereafter BBC WAC]; Dorothy Macardle, "On a California Campus," *Alexandra College Magazine*, vol. 9 (December 1939), 14–17. Reprinted in *Mills Quarterly* 23:8–9, May 1940.

48  Rosalind A. Keep, *Fourscore Years: A History of Mills College* (Oakland: Mills College, 1931), 106–37; Dorothy Macardle, "On a California Campus," *Mills Quarterly* 23: 8–9, May 1940.

poverty, hunger, disease, and crime," and "world-mindedness [was] humanity's most vehement need." She discussed the humanitarian achievements of the League of Nations, such as its work in fighting epidemics and drug trafficking, to illustrate the importance of international cooperation. She alluded to the European political situation, adding that it was vital for people to speak out against evil; public opinion, when forcefully expressed, could lead oppressive governments to reconsider their policies.[49] She believed that the force of American public opinion had been crucial to Ireland in its War of Independence. Dorothy praised America, and urged Americans to collectively stand for freedom and justice, and denounce inhumanity. The college awarded her an Honorary Doctorate of Humane Letters.[50]

Her visit to America in the spring of 1939 had seemed like a holiday, with "old Europe and its cares forgotten," but she was to be confronted by various political crises when she returned to Europe in July.[51] The IRA, now led by the right-wing Seán Russell, was in the midst of a bombing campaign in England. The IRA campaign, however, paled in comparison to the violence that was about to come. Dorothy was in London when Adolf Hitler invaded Poland on September 1, 1939, and war was declared two days later.

49 "The Common Enemy," Commencement Address Delivered by Miss Dorothy Macardle, Monday, June 12, 1939, Mills College Archive, Oakland, California.
50 Macardle, "The Common Enemy;" Macardle, "On a California Campus," 9. See also the articles in Paul Weindling, ed. *International Health Organisations and Movements, 1918–1939* (Cambridge, Cambridge University Press, 1995), for the League of Nations' work in fighting disease and social ills.
51 Macardle, "On a California Campus," 9.

CHAPTER SIX

# Wartime London and the BBC

OROTHY SPENT THE duration of World War II in
England, where she took part in humanitarian work and
journalism in addition to writing novels. She first lived with
her youngest brother Donald and his wife Enid in Sussex, and then in
a series of her own apartments in London. Donald, a theatrical
manager and actor, had become a successful novelist by the 1940s,
specializing in coming-of-age novels about young girls, and one of his
novels was filmed. Dorothy disliked living in England, where all of
her siblings lived, but wanted to remain there during the war to contribute in some way to the struggle against Fascism, mainly through
journalism and humanitarian work.[1] Dorothy described herself as
someone who was in the war "not simply to defend home and
country, but because of the ideas which they believe to be at stake."[2]

Ireland, under Éamon de Valera's leadership, remained neutral
during the war despite intense negotiation and pressure from Britain
to join. By successfully pursuing an independent policy of neutrality,
Ireland demonstrated that it was a sovereign state in all but name.
During the "Emergency," neutrality was maintained in part through

1 RJD, NLI MS 32,582 (96), 20 August 1941. According to Dorothy's god-
daughter, she had moved to London to be near her sister and brothers, although
her relationships with them were not especially close. Ann Keating to author, 14
June 2004. Donald's novels include *Summer in April* (Philadelphia: Lippincott,
1946).
2 Script Outline, "What is the Enemy?," Dorothy Macardle File, BBC WAC, n.d.
[1941].

strict censorship of news, and films which might sway public opinion on the war were banned as well. Due to restrictions on imports, Ireland experienced shortages of food and fuel, though these shortages were less severe than elsewhere in wartime Europe. The government promoted rationing and conservation and a tillage campaign to enable the population to cope with shortages. Concerned that IRA activity would provide a pretext for Britain to invade Ireland, the government passed strict legislation to deal with the IRA, allowing for internment, and, in some cases, execution. Irish neutrality tilted towards Britain and the Allies, with, for instance, aid given to Allied airmen. Although Partition had been one of the main points of contention in Anglo-Irish relations, the existence of Northern Ireland was crucially important in allowing Ireland to remain neutral, as the Allies had Northern Irish naval and air bases at their disposal and refrained from trying to seize the Treaty ports or invade Éire (southern Ireland).[3] Dorothy, despite her republicanism, was initially ambivalent about the neutrality policy.

In 1940, after a period of "phony war," the Second World War began in earnest for the people of Britain. By June 1940, the Low Countries and France had fallen to the Nazis, while Britain continued to hold out. Dorothy performed relief work on behalf of Central and Eastern European refugees in London who had fled their Nazi-occupied countries, and came to know many of them well, such as a Polish Jewish doctor and her young son.[4] She witnessed the chaos and trauma of the Blitz, when the Luftwaffe bombed London on nightly raids in late 1940, but her own apartment building in Kensington escaped destruction.[5] While Dorothy emerged unscathed from Nazi bombing, *The Irish Republic* was not so lucky. The warehouse in which it was stored took a direct hit, and all the stocks were destroyed, to her great regret, as she knew a reprint would be impossible during the war due to paper shortages. "Eight years writing and four years selling!" she lamented.[6] However, the book

---

3 K. Theodore Hoppen, *Ireland Since 1800: Conflict and Conformity* (London: Longman, 1989), 184–5. The Treaty ports were ports in southern Ireland that Britain had retained as part of the 1921 Anglo-Irish Treaty, but had returned following negotiations between de Valera and British Prime Minister Neville Chamberlain in 1938.
4 *Alexandra College Magazine*, vol. 10 (December 1944), 32; RJD, NLI MS 32,582 (115), 25 August 1945.
5 Dorothy Macardle File, BBC WAC, 26 November 1941.
6 Dorothy Macardle to the BBC, Dorothy Macardle File, BBC WAC, 12 June 1941.

rose from its own ashes and was reprinted numerous times after the war.

In 1941, while working on her first novel, she broke into scriptwriting for the BBC, and began giving broadcasts shortly afterwards. Dorothy's interest in writing for and broadcasting on the BBC had begun in the late 1930s. Before leaving for her American tour, she wrote to the BBC requesting an audition, as she hoped to give a broadcast entitled "An Irishwoman Sees the World." She mentioned that she had given frequent radio talks in Dublin, mainly on Irish literature and drama, and that she had an indeterminate accent. "I am regarded in England as speaking with a slight brogue and in Ireland as being afflicted with an Oxford accent,"[7] she noted. It seems that this broadcast never took place, and Dorothy did not work with the BBC for two more years. At that time, a BBC staff member supported her application to broadcast on the North American Service, commenting that Americans were less likely than British listeners to notice Dorothy's "slight Irish accent." Her "strong Irish republican ... but extremely anti-Nazi" political stance "considerably enhance[d] her value as an objective speaker about present-day England for the North American audience." Dorothy's ideas for radio talks included a discussion of relief efforts, funded by American donations, on behalf of children in England affected by Nazi air raids. Her application was successful, and Dorothy gave her first North American Service broadcast in July 1941.[8]

Dorothy wrote a script entitled "What is the Enemy?," for the BBC's North American Services Department in June 1941, which illuminated her political outlook at the time. Liberal democracy was what she cherished most, and race domination was what she most strenuously opposed. She had struggled against British domination in her native Ireland, and hoped India would one day be free of British rule. Now, however, Germany was the major proponent of the ideology of racial dominance, and Britain its leading opponent. She wished Ireland, with its democratic outlook, could join Britain in the war against the Nazis, but due to the 1921 Anglo-Irish Treaty and

---

7 Dorothy Macardle to the BBC, Dorothy Macardle File, BBC WAC, 3 March 1939.
8 "Talks for North America," BBC Internal Circulating Memo, Dorothy Macardle File, BBC WAC, 29 May 1941. A note on the memo says "One talk, Wed/Thurs 2/3 July."

5. Dorothy Macardle,
early 1940s.
(Source: *New York
Times*, 1942)

continuing anger over Partition, this could not happen. "British Statesmen missed a glorious opportunity in December 1921," she maintained, and it was "a pity this mistake has to be paid for today, and not by England alone."[9] She opposed conscripting Northern Irish nationalists, as it could only exacerbate nationalist resentment and worsen British-Irish relations.[10] Dorothy's script demonstrates how she could be politically useful in presenting the rightness of the British case to American audiences; even an opponent of British rule and Partition was insisting that in the current conflict, Britain had right on its side.

Dorothy's work with the BBC linked her to two other Irish women writers in London at the time, Kate O'Brien and Elizabeth Bowen. Kate O'Brien, like Dorothy, was a UCD graduate who had been raised in a wealthy Catholic family in a provincial Irish town. Her

9 Dorothy Macardle, Outline of a Script Entitled "What is the Enemy?," Dorothy Macardle File, BBC WAC [June 1941].
10 Dorothy Macardle, "Conscription in North Ireland," *New Statesman and Nation*, 24 May 1941, 533.

novels "were deceptively traditional in form but radical in content – each novel a Trojan horse smuggling in forbidden topics such as adultery, lesbianism, and venereal disease through the medium of her civilized, graceful narratives."[11] O'Brien broadcast book reviews for the BBC Home Service, as well as giving broadcasts as part of her work for the Ministry of Information.[12] Elizabeth Bowen, who came from a wealthy Irish Protestant family with an ancestral home in County Cork, wrote masterful short stories as well as novels. She gave broadcasts on the BBC in the 1940s, and, like Dorothy, was an accomplished journalist and drama critic. During World War II, she worked as an air raid warden in London. Bowen also worked for the British Ministry of Information, and visited Ireland in the early stages of the conflict to report on Irish public opinion regarding the war and the possible use of the southern Irish Treaty ports by the British navy. She spoke with politicians, journalists, and writers, and addressed the Irish Women Writers' Club on "characterization in f-f-fiction."[13] Dorothy was in England at the time and may never have met Bowen, but she met O'Brien at the Women Writers' Club.

Dorothy's stance during the war links her with some Irish republicans and differentiates her from others. In the mid–1930s, the IRA newspaper *An Phoblacht* denounced Nazism, reflecting the leftist views held by many of its members. By the time war broke out in 1939, the organization, now led by the Chief of Staff and Nazi sympathizer Seán Russell, had changed. Most of its older and more progressive members, such as Peadar O'Donnell and George Gilmore, had resigned, and younger, right-wing or apolitical members gained greater prominence. During World War II, the IRA was a marginal organization with a number of Nazi sympathizers as well as militarists who supported Nazi Germany for strategic reasons, believing that a British defeat at the hands of the Nazis would give Ireland greater leverage to end Partition.[14] Republicans within Fianna Fáil

11  Éibhear Walshe, *Kate O'Brien, A Writing Life* (Dublin: Irish Academic Press, 2006), 2.
12  Walshe, *Kate O'Brien*, 98.
13  Victoria Glendinning, *Elizabeth Bowen* (New York: Alfred A. Knopf, 1978), 98, 145–6, 159–60, 202–4, 255–6; R.F. Foster, "The Irishness of Elizabeth Bowen," in Foster, *Paddy and Mr. Punch* (Oxford: Oxford University Press, 1993), 102–22. For Bowen's talk at the Women Writers' Club meeting, where Rosamond Jacob noticed her characteristic stammer, see RJD, NLI 32,582 (90), 6 December 1939.
14  Brian Hanley, *The IRA 1926–1936* (Dublin: Four Courts Press, 2002), 184–5, 197–8; Fearghal McGarry, *Frank Ryan* (Dundalk: Dundalgan Press, 2002), 66.

tended to support the government's neutrality policy while favouring the Allies rather than the Nazis, and opposed IRA activity that could jeopardize neutrality by provoking British intervention in Ireland. Dorothy's friends were mostly progressive Irish nationalists now in their forties and fifties who opposed Hitler. Rosamond Jacob, for instance, a self-described republican pacifist, supported Irish neutrality and had long been an opponent of Nazism.[15]

In England, Dorothy defended Irish neutrality throughout the war, but was privately more ambivalent about Ireland's policy in the early stages of the conflict. On a visit to Ireland in August 1941, she told friends that she thought Ireland should turn over the Treaty ports for British use if the United States entered the war. A year later, she said Ireland should ask for British and American help if the Nazis announced they were going to invade Ireland.[16] She became more sympathetic to Irish neutrality later in the war, though she wished Ireland could have joined with the democracies. In early 1944, she felt "with equal intensity the wish that we were in a position to help with this war, & the conviction that we have a right to stay out of it." Although she had been favourably impressed by America during her tour in 1939, she now felt hostility towards the "powerful, rich, and populous" United States for "stay[ing] out of the fighting until [its] own territory was attacked," adding that she was "miserably disillusioned."[17] Dorothy also worried about the way Ireland's position was misrepresented in the British and American media.[18] However, she was pleased by the representation of Ireland's political position in an American "March of Time" film, *The Irish Question*, as it showed the Irish people's support for neutrality.[19] By 1945, she had become a

15 RJD, NLI MS 32,582 (90), 31 December 1939.
16 RJD, NLI MS 32,582 (96), 20 August 1941; RJD, NLI MS 32,582 (100), 26 August 1942. This suggests she may have worked for the British Ministry of Information in some capacity, as her line of questioning was similar to Elizabeth Bowen's, although no record has been found. Bowen noted that her work for the Ministry enabled her to travel to Ireland when wartime travel bans were in place. Glendinning, 202. In June 1944, Dorothy, in England, wrote to an Irish friend about how pleased she was to hear of the possibility that the travel ban might be lifted. Dorothy Macardle to Kathleen O'Connell, UCDA P155/127 (5), 16 June 1944.
17 Dorothy Macardle to Frank Gallagher, Frank Gallagher Papers, NLI MS 18,340, 13 March 1944.
18 Macardle to Gallagher, Frank Gallagher Papers, NLI MS 18,340, 2 April 1944.
19 Dorothy Macardle to Kathleen O'Connell, UCDA P155/127 (5), 16 June 1944. For a review of *The Irish Question*, see "Film Notes," *Irish Times*, 4 September 1944.

strong defender of the Fianna Fáil government's policy of neutrality, and praised Éamon de Valera for his statesmanship. In her view, neutrality prevented the destabilization of Ireland, which could have undermined the Allies, and successfully maintaining an independent policy had made Ireland, for all intents and purposes, a fully sovereign, independent republic.[20]

Dorothy also contributed scripts to the BBC's Schools Broadcasting Department. She wrote a script on the life of St Patrick for the History Series in November 1941. The program was produced by Rhoda Power, the sister of Eileen Power, the famous LSE economic historian. Prior to Eileen's death in 1940, the Power sisters had sometimes collaborated on history textbooks and history programs broadcast to schoolchildren.[21] Jean Sutcliffe, another member of the Department, produced a Christmas play Dorothy wrote for the Under Nines Series in December 1941. Sutcliffe valued her contributions to the Department, and Dorothy, in turn, enjoyed writing for schoolchildren and admired the professionalism of the Schools Broadcasting staff.[22]

In 1942 Dorothy gave a series of monthly broadcasts on the BBC's North American Service, for which she was paid twelve guineas each. She spoke to North American audiences about the experiences of children in various countries under Nazi occupation, such as Norway and Czechoslovakia. She recorded her talks late at night so that North American audiences could listen in the early evening. Dorothy researched stories by conducting interviews in the refugee hostels where she volunteered, and by visiting a school for Czech children. She also spoke with representatives from the Czechoslovak government-in-exile's Department of Information. Laurence Gilliam, the head of the Features Department, ran a series called "Escape to Freedom." Dorothy dramatized a story for the series about Norwegians escaping their country, in addition to giving a talk on Norway for the North American Service.[23]

20  Dorothy Macardle, "Without Fanfares: Some Reflections on the Republic of Éire," *The Commonweal*, 30 November 1945, 161–4.
21  Dorothy Macardle File, BBC WAC; Maxine Berg, *A Woman in History: Eileen Power, 1889–1940* (Cambridge: Cambridge University Press, 1996), 230–4. See also R.C. Steele, "Broadcasting to Schools," in *BBC Handbook 1941* (London, 1941), 89–93.
22  Dorothy Macardle File, BBC WAC.
23  RJD, NLI MS 32,582 (99), 26 July 1942; Dorothy Macardle File, BBC WAC;

Life in wartime England enabled Dorothy to think and write about her early experiences of family and her troubled relationship with a mother whose memory still haunted her. She restaged her relationship with Minnie in various guises in the novels she wrote between 1941 and 1953. Dorothy worked on her first novel, *Uneasy Freehold*, during the early stages of World War II, and used a ghost story plot and Gothic conventions to frame a narrative about troubled marriages and parent-child relationships, family secrets, violence, and problematic sexuality.[24] The novel does, however, have a happy ending.

The "female Gothic" genre emerged in novels and film by the early 1940s. Daphne du Maurier's *Rebecca* (1938) and Dorothy Macardle's *Uneasy Freehold* (1941) were two of the most popular female Gothic novels of the period, and both were adapted for the screen in the early 1940s. Dorothy, then, played a significant role in defining a popular new literary and cinematic genre. The female Gothic genre "involves the haunting of a woman by another woman (usually a rival, a Doppelganger, or a mother) and/or by her own projected sexual fears [and] anxieties about transgressive sexuality."[25] The doppelganger, in Gothic novels, is a double or a "second self" who shadows the protagonist. Ghosts or doppelgangers are often destroyed or erased at the novel's conclusion, allowing the protagonist to move on.[26] Symbolic doubles, like ghosts, may represent the manifestation of a seemingly normal woman's fears of deviance and monstrosity. Female Gothic novels and films feature "the interrelated themes of investigation, paranoia, and (usually deviant) sexuality," as the protagonist, usually female, investigates the mystery behind supernatural occurrences. The setting of the investigation tends to be a haunted house where a "monstrous act" took place or where an evil and transgressive

---

Sian Nicholas, *The Echo of War: Home Front Propaganda and the Wartime BBC, 1939–45* (Manchester: Manchester University Press, 1996), 158.

24 Her novels included *Uneasy Freehold* (London: Peter Davies, 1941); *Fantastic Summer* (London: Peter Davies, 1946); and *Dark Enchantment* (Garden City, New York: Doubleday, 1953). Her second novel, *The Seed Was Kind* (London: Peter Davies, 1944), did not deal with the supernatural. The American edition of *Uneasy Freehold* was retitled *The Uninvited*, and all of the following references are to the American edition.

25 Misha Kavka, "The Gothic on Screen," in Jerrold E. Hogle, ed., *The Cambridge Companion to Gothic Fiction* (New York: Cambridge University Press, 2002), 219.

26 Avril Horner and Sue Zlosnik, *Daphne du Maurier: Writing, Identity, and the Gothic Imagination* (Basingstoke: Macmillan Press, 1998), 119, 128.

woman once lived.[27] Gothic novels also reveal women's fears of repression and confinement; early Gothic novels, for instance, featured young heroines imprisoned in dungeons by cruel family members or other dangerous figures until their rescue by the hero.

Writing a supernatural and Gothic novel, rather than a realist one, may have helped Dorothy achieve greater distance from disturbing autobiographical material. While Dorothy's multilayered novels should not simply be seen as reflecting a therapeutic need to resolve her anger towards Minnie through the relentless performance of maternal destruction, female Gothic novels do allow for the metaphorical killing of mothers whose baleful memories haunt their daughters. In light of her problematic relationship with Minnie, this would seem to be important to Dorothy as she considered ways to frame narratives about bad mothers and troubled family relationships, and *Uneasy Freehold* was not her only novel to culminate in symbolic maternal destruction or erasure that allows a daughter to move on.

*Uneasy Freehold* centres on the Fitzgerald siblings, Roderick and Pamela, and their attempt to solve the mystery of a haunted house in Devon they have just purchased. Their investigation leads them to believe that two ghosts, one warm and benevolent and one cold and dangerous, haunt the house. Roderick becomes interested in Stella Meredith, whose parents, artist Llewellyn and his wife Mary, had once lived in the house with Carmel, an artist's model from Spain with whom Llewellyn had been romantically involved. The Merediths and Carmel died when Stella was a child, and the shy, repressed young woman lives in the village with her stern, morbid maternal grandfather. Her grandfather has an unhealthy obsession with Mary's memory, and Stella, like other Gothic heroines, is made a virtual prisoner in the house as he tries to reshape her in Mary's image. Local people inform the Fitzgeralds that Mary was a virtuous, gracious, lady, and that Carmel was temperamental and uncontrolled. The siblings at first think Mary is the warm ghost, and Carmel the cold ghost, but after holding a séance, they realize they were mistaken. Carmel, the warm ghost and Stella's real mother, refused to be silenced and cast aside, instead returning to tell the truth, and Mary, the cold malevolent ghost, tried to prevent the exposure of family secrets.[28] In life, Carmel

27  Kavka, "The Gothic on Screen," 219–20.
28  Family secrets are an important theme in Anglo-Irish Gothic literature. *Uneasy Freehold* relates to some of the conventions of Anglo-Irish Gothic fiction, in

had been a warm and loving mother, and Mary had been cold and cruel. Roderick, Dorothy's alter ego, symbolically kills the evil "mother," banishing Mary's ghost through ridicule, while Stella's acceptance of the truth about her mother's identity allows her to move on and ensures that Carmel will no longer haunt the house. Her grandfather dies, and the novel concludes with Stella's acceptance of Roderick's proposal of marriage.

The novel is written in the first person, with Roderick as the narrator. The child of an Irish father and an English mother, Roderick shares a number of characteristics with Dorothy besides his family background.[29] Both were journalists who wrote dramatic and literary criticism for a newspaper, as well as contemporary history. The thirty-year-old Roderick works on a book called *The History of the British Censorship*, "designed to cause that animal's death by exposure."[30] Dorothy campaigned for years against censorship in Ireland.[31] Both Dorothy and Roderick want to write plays most of all. Dorothy felt that the writing of *The Irish Republic* kept her from concentrating on drama and affected her creativity,[32] while Roderick loses interest in his book on censorship and puts it aside to work on a play called *Barbara*. Like Dorothy, whose novels allude to marital power struggles and feature the erasure of evil maternal figures and other deviant women, Roderick is interested in "exploring unrecognized motives, and I am sure the love of power takes queer twists in women—it is so repressed."[33] Roderick writes a play about an evil woman called Barbara who perversely enjoys goading people to self-destruct, but who is herself destroyed at the end.[34]

Dorothy incorporated lesbianism into the novel as a Gothic element of transgressive sexuality. Miss Holloway, a friend of Mary's who now operates a nursing home, is coded as a lesbian, since she is

---

which "representations of the living dead as ghosts frequently figure a return of repressed or unresolved historical events." Margot Gayle Backus, *The Gothic Family Romance: Heterosexuality, Child Sacrifice, and the Anglo-Irish Colonial Order* (Durham: Duke University Press, 1999), 246.

29 The Fitzgerald siblings are portrayed as upper-middle-class Anglo-Irish Protestants with a vaguely nationalist orientation. Their parents have been dead for some years, and it is implied that their relationship with their father was troubled. Macardle, *The Uninvited*, 3–4, 8–9, 106, 240.

30 Ibid., 4.

31 *Irish Press*, 1 January 1937; RJD, NLI MS 32,582 (97), 17 September 1941.

32 *Irish Press*, 4 February 1938; RJD, NLI MS 32,582 (85), 25 August 1938.

33 Macardle, *The Uninvited*, 282.

34 Ibid., 90–4.

an "unfeminine" spinster who had been infatuated with her friend
Mary and still worships her memory.[35] The nursing home is itself a
Gothic-style prison for the containment of illness and deviance, and
patients seem to lose their autonomy and identities.[36] Dorothy knew
the literary codes well, and sidestepped the censorship of her novel by
not making a lesbian relationship between Miss Holloway and Mary
explicit. Kate O'Brien's novel, *Mary Lavelle*, which features an
openly lesbian character, was found obscene by the Irish censors and
was banned in 1936.[37] Dorothy's characterization of Miss Holloway
may have been influenced by Daphne du Maurier's popular Gothic
novel *Rebecca*, which features an ambiguously lesbian character, Mrs
Danvers, as well as a twist ending showing that a dead icon was not
quite what she seemed.[38]

Dorothy was interested in exploring the impact of the representation and iconization of women on the lives of real women. In
*Uneasy Freehold*, she reworked some of the themes found in her
*Earth-bound* stories. Llewellyn, like Hugo in "The Story of Róisín
Dhu," is a self-absorbed painter, and Carmel is an artist's model like
Nuala who falls in love with the painter. Carmel's appearance
changes for the worse during her unhealthy and exploitative relationship with Llewellyn, and he paints her looking haggard and debased. A
young, beautiful, vibrant woman is transformed into one approaching
death, like Nuala, whose story reversed the Irish myth of an
old woman's rejuvenation, found in Yeats' *Cathleen Ní Houlihan*.
Carmel dies after being sacrificed to Llewellyn's artistic needs, and his
death by drowning follows. Like Hugo, who also drowned, he may
have been haunted by the ghost or memory of his muse. The bonds
between Carmel and her daughter Stella are broken when Stella is raised
to believe that she is Mary's daughter. Llewellyn paints an attractive
portrait of Mary that belies her unattractive personality, and the
portrait is kept in Stella's bedroom. Stella's grandfather presents Mary
as an icon for Stella to live up, and her own life is sacrificed to the

35  This is more explicit in the film; Mary's "unspoken lesbian sexuality" com-
     pounds her "monstrosity," and "the sins of the mother ... take a detour through
     homosexual and antiprocreative deviance before being visited on" Stella. Kavka,
     "The Gothic on Screen," 221.
36  Macardle, *The Uninvited*, 163. The description of the nursing home's atmos-
     phere may reflect the anxiety and frustration Dorothy felt during the many times
     she spent in nursing homes due to illness.
37  Walshe, *Kate O'Brien*, 65–8.
38  Daphne du Maurier, *Rebecca* (London: Victor Gollancz, 1938).

worship of an ideal mother as she too develops a morbid obsession with Mary's memory. When the real Mary behind the portrait is revealed to have been frigid and cruel, and not a mother at all, Stella is able to figuratively restore the bonds with her own mother, overcome the dead weight of the past and false ideals, and move on to independence and adulthood and marriage. Even after death, Carmel refuses silent suffering and removal, and the empowering love of a strong-willed mother overcomes death to allow Stella to rejoin the world of the living, rather than remain obsessed with ghosts.[39]

Dorothy's treatment of female sexuality departed in some ways from its treatment by writers in Ireland in the 1940s. Realist writers, both male and female, depicted female characters in ways that opposed "the Catholic nationalist construction of femininity as both sexually innocent and safely domestic."[40] Irish realist writers such as Seán O'Faoláin and Frank O'Connor wrote stories set in provincial Ireland that featured sexual repression as well as promiscuity and violence, undermining idealized portrayals of rural Ireland. Maura Laverty, a broadcast journalist with Radio Éireann, wrote a popular novel called *Never No More* (1942), which depicted sexually active women in a nostalgic but earthy narrative about life in rural Ireland. Margaret Barrington, in her short story "Village Without Men," comically celebrated the sexual desires of a group of Donegal women.[41] Dorothy's novels, with one exception, did not take place in Ireland, and she often used Gothic devices rather than realist or comic ones as she depicted difficult relationships and problematic sexuality.

*Uneasy Freehold* reflected Dorothy's deep interest in ghost stories, occult phenomena, and Spiritualism. Like her protagonists, she had lived in houses she believed were haunted.[42] She may have attended séances to attempt to communicate with her brother Kenneth, who had been killed in World War I, like countless people who had lost

39 This analysis is indebted to Jennifer Molidor's discussion of the themes of iconization and female self-sacrifice and mother-daughter bonds in the stories in *Earth-bound*, particularly "The Portrait of Roísín Dhu" and "The Return of Niav." Jennifer Molidor, "Violence, Silence, and Sacrifice: the Mother-Daughter Relationship in the Short Fiction of Modern Irish Women Writers, 1890–1980" (PhD Dissertation, Notre Dame University, 2007). I am also grateful to Gerardine Meaney and Luke Gibbons for discussing *Uneasy Freehold* with me, and to Vera Kreilkamp, who commented on an earlier paper on this novel.

40 Clair Wills, "Women Writers and the Death of Rural Ireland: Realism and Nostalgia in the 1940s," *Éire-Ireland* 41:1&2, Spring/Summer 2006, 193.

41 Wills, 192–212.

42 Ann Keating to author, 18 August 2004.

relatives in the war, or heard séances described by friends who took them seriously. During the 1920s and 1930s, Spiritualism, ghosts, and haunted houses were part of British popular culture.[43] Dorothy was aware of recent case studies of alleged hauntings, both as a member of the Society for Psychical Research and as an avid reader of books, newspapers and magazines. Reports of hauntings repeatedly appeared in popular newspapers, gaining widespread attention. For example, in February 1938 the *Sunday Pictorial* reported the story of the Forbes family, who claimed their home in Thornton Heath was being violently disturbed by poltergeists. This led to extensive media coverage, and psychical researchers joined in the fray. One researcher later concluded that Mrs Forbes was mentally unbalanced and had created the disturbances.[44]

*Uneasy Freehold* was both a commercial and critical success. It was first published in Britain in 1941, and an American edition, retitled *The Uninvited*, was published in 1942. The novel, which sold half a million copies,[45] was widely reviewed in Britain and in the United States. Novelist Leonora Eyles, in the *Times Literary Supplement*, declared *Uneasy Freehold* "a perfect escape novel" and "the ideal ghost story," adding that "the author writes with such conviction as to make the story quite credible; above all, she writes with a curious under-standing of and pity for the ghosts who are, quite obviously, as real to her as the flesh and blood people in her tale."[46] A *New York Times* reviewer also liked the characters and commended the "clever and original" plot. She found the resolution satisfactory, but noted that "any ghost story with a supernatural solution will not quite satisfy the completely materialistic."[47] Another critic thought that "Miss Macardle seems unduly feminine while writing in the first person as Roddy ... there is a 'Rebecca' like twist that is a trifle too obvious and ... 'The Uninvited' has no more claims to being serious literature than 'Rebecca' had." Nevertheless, it was an outstanding example of the

43 Jenny Hazelgrove, *Spiritualism and British Society Between the Wars* (Manchester: Manchester University Press, 2000), 28.

44 Hazelgrove, 175–7.

45 Peter Tremayne, "A Reflection of Ghosts," in Stephen Jones and Jo Fletcher, eds., *Gaslight and Ghosts* (London: Robinson, 1988), 86–7. The British edition sold for eight shillings, sixpence, while the American one cost $2.50.

46 Leonora Eyles, review of *Uneasy Freehold* by Dorothy Macardle, *Times Literary Supplement*, 14 February 1942, 81.

47 Charlotte Dean, review of *The Uninvited* by Dorothy Macardle, *New York Times*, 26 July 1942, Section VI, 6.

ghost story genre.[48] *The Uninvited* was significant at the time in demonstrating the commercial potential of ghost stories, and the "unashamedly excessive sentimentality" of the film helped set the stage for other ghost movies and novels in the 1940s.[49]

Paramount Pictures bought the film rights to *The Uninvited*, and the film version was released in the United States and in Britain in early 1944. Due to the war, it was filmed in California rather than on location in southern England. It was adapted for the screen by the English writer Dodie Smith, best known for *101 Dalmations*, who was then living in Hollywood. *The Uninvited*, directed by Lewis Allen, featured Ray Milland as Roderick, Ruth Hussey as Pamela, Gail Russell as Stella, and Cornelia Otis Skinner as Miss Holloway. A *New York Times* reviewer, who described *The Uninvited* as a "black-and-white melodrama," noted that the film demonstrated Hollywood's new interest in the unconscious and in the dreams and apparitions that had played an important role in avant-garde European films.[50] When *The Uninvited* opened in London, the *Times* reviewer described it as "a conventional 'thriller' with a wicked ghost taking the part of the sinister villain." The critic was bemused by Hollywood's conception of Cornwall, where the film was set.[51]

By the summer of 1944, the film was playing in Irish theatres. Dorothy's friend Rosamond Jacob went to see *The Uninvited* at Dublin's Theatre de Luxe on Camden Street in August. She thought it was a "very good film tho of course much changed from the book. No ghost anywhere visible—only formless mist once or twice— should have been sight of Mary M in the end."[52] Another individual, far more prominent in Ireland than Jacob, also saw the film and commented upon it. Éamon de Valera, who watched *The Uninvited* at the Savoy on O'Connell Street with his staff members Kathleen O'Connell and Maurice Moynihan, was struck by the twist ending, in which "the good [Mary] was bad, and the bad [Carmel] was good," and commented "typical Dorothy." He thought that the

48 Orville Prescott, "Books of the Times," *New York Times*, 27 July 1942. He was referring to Daphne du Maurier's popular novel *Rebecca* (London: Gollancz, 1938).
49 Brian Stableford, "Dorothy Macardle," in David Pringle, ed., *St James Guide to Horror, Ghost, and Gothic Writers* (Detroit: St James Press, 1998), 381.
50 Bosley Crowther, "The Screen," *New York Times*, 26 February 1944, 3.
51 "New Films in London," *Times*, 3 April 1944, 8.
52 RJD, NLI MS 32,582 (110), 22 August 1944.

moral of *The Uninvited* was meant for him, and that Dorothy was still angry about the 1937 Constitution.[53] *The Uninvited* undermined assumptions about good and bad mothers reflected in the Constitution,[54] since in the novel and film, Carmel, a strong and loving unmarried mother, trumps Mary, a married "mother" whose outward display of moral rectitude conceals coldness and cruelty, in the moral stakes. Furthermore, Mary, to outward appearances the idealized, virtuous, domestic mother extolled by church and state and the framers of the Constitution, may well be a lesbian. Dorothy showed complexity and transgression behind simplistic ideals of womanhood, and Roderick's banishment of Mary through ridicule can be viewed as mocking the ideal of the virtuous mother promoted by the Constitution, as well as metaphorically killing a problematic maternal figure.

Dorothy was not entirely pleased with the film. She lamented that "the British censor took out the ghosts [in the American version of the film a ghost with a clearly visible woman's face is shown], and what's left is rather lacking in logic! ... Scarcely two words of mine survive. In America the audience screamed; it is considered a huge success, and Paramount are trying to make me write a shocker for them. I decline to become a 'shocker writer' and they are grieved ... I don't feel it's my vocation to add to the horrific elements in the world today."[55] During a visit to Dublin that autumn, Dorothy gave a lecture on film adaptations of novels. She felt that novels were ruined when they were adapted for the screen, because they were thoroughly changed and simplified. This occurred "because producing a film costs so much that to make a profit they arrange it to suit the lowest mentality of tired unthinking millions."[56]

*Uneasy Freehold* is significant for shedding light on a number of Dorothy's preoccupations. Her interest in Spiritualism and the occult demonstrated that she took part in contemporary cultural debates that took place in Britain as well as Ireland. She contributed to the literary history of the period by reworking Gothic and occult conventions and infusing them with a new energy that gave them

53  Tim Pat Coogan, *De Valera, Long Fellow, Long Shadow* (London, 1995), 500.
54  My thanks to Luke Gibbons for pointing out how *Uneasy Freehold* can be seen as a response to the Constitution. Luke Gibbons, conversation with author, 5 October 2006.
55  Dorothy Macardle to Kathleen O'Connell, Kathleen O'Connell Papers, UCDA P155/127 (5), 16 June 1944.
56  RJD, NLI MS 32,582 (111), 21 October 1944.

popular and commercial appeal. She revisited the theme of the gulf between idealized images of womanhood and real women's lives. Lastly, the novel allowed her to explore some of her own feelings about mothers, including her own, and dysfunctional families.

Dorothy returned to Ireland for several short periods during the war. During a visit in November 1944, she became embroiled in a controversy regarding the compulsory Irish language policy in the schools. Czechoslovak Foreign Affairs Minister Jan Masaryk was in Dublin to lecture at Trinity College, and the Fianna Fáil newspaper, the *Irish Press*, marked the occasion by running an editorial praising the successful Czech language revival and comparing it to the revival of Irish.[57] Ironically, an outside expert on education, the Czech educationalist Johanna Pollak, had in 1943 conducted a study of the compulsory Irish policy in the schools, and concluded that the policy was not working. The Czech language revival was far more successful. Pollak's assessment matched that of a 1942 report by INTO (the Irish National Teacher's Organization), and was therefore shelved by a Fianna Fáil government ideologically committed to compulsory Irish.[58] Dorothy, a former teacher who opposed compulsory Irish for pedagogical reasons, wrote a letter to the *Irish Press* praising Czechoslovakia and outlining its educational philosophy, which did not involve forcing Czech language immersion on children who were not native speakers.[59] She herself was writing a booklet on Czech education for the Czech government-in-exile. The *Irish Press* editor attacked Dorothy on several minor points in her letters, and repeatedly insisted she was mistaken.[60]

Other letters followed,[61] demonstrating the heightened sensitivity and defensiveness of some supporters of compulsory Irish at a time when the policy was generating serious opposition. Dorothy held her ground, maintaining that the policy might eventually "defeat its own ends."[62] The *Irish Press* soon became less enthusiastic about Masaryk

---

57  "Parallels," *Irish Press*, 3 November 1944.
58  Adrian Kelly, *Compulsory Irish: Language and Education in Ireland 1870s–1970s* (Dublin: Irish Academic Press, 2002), 49–53.
59  Dorothy Macardle to the *Irish Press*, 8 November 1944.
60  Dorothy Macardle to the *Irish Press*, 9 November 1944; *Irish Press*, 8–9 November 1944. See also Dorothy Macardle and M. Sargantova, *Educating a Free People* (London: Trinity Press, 1945).
61  See the letters to the *Irish Press*, 15–22 November 1944. A collection of the correspondence is contained in NAI, D/TAOIS s7801A.
62  Dorothy Macardle to the *Irish Press*, 24 November 1944.

and his country when Éamon de Valera prevented him from speaking to the Irish Institute of International Affairs, to which Dorothy had once belonged. De Valera believed that the Institute was composed of propagandists opposed to Irish neutrality who invited speakers to attack the course taken by the Fianna Fáil government.[63]

Nostalgic memoirs became popular in Britain and Ireland during World War II, as those living in a world of violence and uncertainty turned to literature to escape to a more stable past, real or imagined.[64] Autobiographical writing about childhood and adolescence could be a way for writers to take stock of their lives in a time of crisis. The Irish writer and Oxford academic Enid Starkie, for instance, wrote *A Lady's Child* at this time, a narrative of her unhappy childhood and adolescence in a wealthy Catholic Unionist family in Edwardian Dublin.[65] The closest Dorothy came to writing a memoir was her most personal novel, *The Seed Was Kind* (1944), a semi-autobiographical work that restaged her conflict with her mother. The novel's depiction of the protagonist's traumatic first sexual experience may also have been based on an incident in Dorothy's own life. Although *The Seed Was Kind* is set in England during the early stages of World War II, rather than in the Edwardian era of Dorothy's youth, the protagonist is partly based on the young Dorothy Macardle. *The Seed Was Kind* depicts a disastrous marriage, a problematic mother-daughter relationship, and a young woman's traumatic sexual experience in realistic terms, unmediated by Gothic or supernatural devices.

The novel focuses on a young English woman named Diony, who resembles Dorothy, and her relationship with a Czech refugee, Karel, in wartime London. Diony and Karel first meet in Geneva in 1937, where they are attending a League of Nations program for students, just as Dorothy had attended lectures there in the summer of 1937. Diony's paternal grandparents live in Geneva, as her French grandfather is a diplomat, while Diony lives in London with her widowed mother, Sybil.[66] Diony, who like Dorothy is a serious, idealistic, liberal internationalist and opponent of Fascism and appeasement,

63  "Taoiseach on Activities of Propagandist Group," *Irish Press*, 10 November 1944. See also de Valera's explanation in *Dáil Debates*, vol. 95, cols. 926–934, 9 November 1944.

64  Wills, "Women Writers and the Death of Rural Ireland," 205–6; Foster, "The Irishness of Elizabeth Bowen," 117; Glendinning, *Elizabeth Bowen*, 200.

65  Enid Starkie, *A Lady's Child* (London: Faber and Faber, 1941).

66  Dorothy Macardle, *The Seed Was Kind* (London: Peter Davies, 1944), 3–5, 21, 29.

clashes with her superficial, self-absorbed mother. Her grandparents also resent Sybil, whom they blame for the failure of her marriage, which ended with her husband Pierre's probable suicide.[67] Diony and Karel meet in London again during the war, as Karel and his violinist cousin Toni are both living there as refugees, and Diony, like Dorothy, volunteers to work with refugees, as well as with the Red Cross.

Diony's infatuation for Karel grows, but he seems preoccupied with politics and ignores her, leaving her feeling humiliated.[68] On a night of heavy bombing during the Blitz in 1940, Diony hears that the deeply depressed and anxious Toni may be suicidal. She rushes to his residence to rescue him before he can overdose on sleeping pills. Despairing that Karel will never return her love, she gives into Toni's sexual demands.[69] Once again, a woman sacrifices herself for a self-centered artist figure. Later, Karel learns what happened and praises Diony for her selflessness. He reveals that he had always been interested in her, but had felt she was superior to him, as she was the grand-daughter of a distinguished diplomat. He asks her to marry him, and the exhilarated Diony agrees, adding that she can volunteer with the Red Cross in Czechoslovakia when Karel chooses to return there.[70]

The novel indicates that Dorothy may have been grappling with guilt about her lingering hostility towards her dead mother, which she tried to resolve. Sybil, who shares some of Minnie's qualities, is portrayed as an utterly hateful failed wife and mother. Her husband and daughter had been afraid of her temper, and Pierre is presented as Sybil's hapless victim, manipulated into marrying her when she lied to him that she was pregnant. Besides having an uncongenial personality and engaging in unconventional sexual behaviour, Sybil fails to support her serious, idealistic daughter's beliefs and goals, mocking Diony's moral earnestness and "puritanical" views regarding sexuality. Diony, during her difficult childhood, wished for a loving family life while coping with her resentment towards Sybil. A friend and her grandmother help her to resolve her guilt. Diony's friend reassures her that it is perfectly all right to dislike Sybil, whose values she cannot respect. Her grandmother blames Sybil when Diony tells

67 Ibid., 117.
68 Ibid., 120–167, 182–5.
69 Ibid., 196–217. This incident particularly bemused Rosamond Jacob, who felt it was a "queer thing for a prude like D. to put in – she has *very* antiquated notions." RJD, NLI MS 32,582 (100), 26 August 1942.
70 Macardle, *The Seed Was Kind*, 220–3.

her about Toni, remarking that Sybil taught Diony "not to trust her finest instincts."[71] Dorothy symbolically banished the memory of an inadequate mother in *Uneasy Freehold*, when Roderick used ridicule to cast out Mary's ghost. In *The Seed Was Kind*, Diony accepts her negative feelings towards her mother, severs ties with her, and moves on to marry the man she loves. However, Dorothy had not completely exorcised the haunting spirit of Minnie Macardle, and their conflict was to be rehearsed twice more.

Overall, *The Seed Was Kind*, Dorothy's least successful novel, stood apart from her other fiction in that it did not use Gothic and occult conventions to grapple with the familiar problematic themes of troubled marriages and mother-daughter relationships and female sexuality. As a heavily political work of fiction, it is also significant for its insights into Dorothy's thinking about World War II from a civilian's perspective.

The Second World War ended in Europe with an Allied victory in May 1945. After six years of living in England, where she wrote two novels, worked for the BBC, and helped refugees, Dorothy was ready to return to Ireland.

71  Ibid., 152.

CHAPTER SEVEN

# Postwar Ireland, *Fantastic Summer,* and *Children of Europe*

D OROTHY ARRIVED IN Ireland in June 1945. For those returning after a long absence in wartime England, Ireland seemed almost unreal at first. Novelist Kate O'Brien, who arrived back in Dublin at about the same time as Dorothy, felt she had travelled far back in time.[1] Dorothy thought "Ireland seemed very quiet, the air very soft, the people gentle in an old-fashioned way."[2] Over the next four years, she wrote a supernatural novel set in Ireland and another work of contemporary history.

During the summer of 1945, Dorothy moved back into her Dundrum home, Creevagh, where she wrote *Fantastic Summer,* her only novel with an Irish setting.[3] Like *Uneasy Freehold*, it dealt with the supernatural. The main character, Virgilia Wilde, is a widow in her early forties with one daughter, Nan. Virgilia, who has lived for years in England, decides to return home to Ireland, and purchases a cottage in Glencree, County Wicklow, in the summer of 1938.[4] Virgilia is partly based on Dorothy. Both Dorothy and Virgilia are

---

1 Éibhear Walshe, *Kate O'Brien, A Writing Life* (Dublin: Irish Academic Press, 2006), 109.
2 Dorothy Macardle, "Without Fanfares, Some Reflections on the Republic of Éire," *The Commonweal,* 30 November 1945, 161–4.
3 RJD, NLI MS 32,582 (115), 26 June 1945, 25 August 1945.
4 Dorothy Macardle, *Fantastic Summer* (London: Peter Davies Ltd., 1946), 19–25.

graduates of Alexandra College, where they were involved in drama, and both lived in Dundrum and Wicklow. Like Dorothy, Virgilia is described as tall and slender, with blue eyes.[5] Dorothy's best friend Linda Kearns MacWhinney, to whom the novel was dedicated, also contributed to the characterization of Virgilia, as both Linda and Virgilia were single mothers with one daughter, while Dorothy was unmarried and childless. Linda had separated from her husband Charles MacWhinney, an engineer like the fictional Henry Wilde, and she lived with their daughter Ann in Dublin.

Virgilia becomes troubled by her psychic powers, including her ability to predict future events, and fears that she may be suffering a mental breakdown. She consults Dr Barnard Franks, a Dublin psychiatrist, who like Virgilia endured an unhappy marriage. Virgilia knew his late wife, Suzette, and still has nightmares about a childhood incident in which Suzette pulled her hair and gave her a violent shaking.[6] Dr Franks reassures Virgilia that she has no psychiatric disorder.[7] Nan soon becomes romantically involved with the psychiatrist's son, Perry, a young doctor with an interest in psychical research who wants Virgilia's visions recorded and publicized to advance scientific understanding. Virgilia takes a dislike to Perry, as he resembles his mother and has a quick temper, and fears he will harm or kill her daughter. She has a frightening vision of Nan being strangled by Perry.[8] At the novel's conclusion, Virgilia senses that Nan is in danger, and sees her being forcibly restrained by a man. However, the man turns out to be Nan's deranged former boyfriend, and Perry is there to rescue her.[9]

Virgilia realizes that while she may be clairvoyant, her supernatural ability is not infallible, and is prone to psychological distortion.[10] She had always been haunted by the memory of Perry's dreadful mother abusing her, and, through transference, unconsciously believed that

---

5  Ibid., 8–13.
6  Dorothy may have had nightmares about violent hair-pulling, as one account of her forced removal from Kilmainham says she was dragged by her hair. Annie Hogan, *Éire*, 19 May 1923. Cited in Sinéad McCoole, *No Ordinary Women: Irish Female Activists in the Revolutionary Years* (Dublin: O'Brien Press, 2003), 123.
7  Macardle, *Fantastic Summer*, 39–48,66.
8  Ibid., 61–62, 76, 101, 107, 244–5.
9  Ibid., 271.
10 For a similar story of preconceptions influencing the interpretation of a vision, told to Dorothy by Maud Gonne MacBride (who believed she had supernatural powers), see Dorothy Macardle, "They Say It Happened," Broadcast Talk, RTÉ Written Archives, 31 October 1955.

Perry would harm Nan in turn. She tells the other characters about Suzette's early treatment of her, and "in the outburst of laughter that followed, the memory of Suzette dissolved."[11] Virgilia is finally able to embrace Perry as her future son-in-law. Just as Roderick in *Uneasy Freehold* disempowers and banishes Mary's ghost through ridicule, the memory of Suzette can no longer haunt the characters in *Fantastic Summer,* and cast a pall over their lives, the moment they realize they will "never be able to think of her again without laughing."[12] Once again, Dorothy's preoccupations are played out when the ghost or memory of an evil maternal figure is made to disappear so that the characters can move on with their lives. Although Virgilia's relationship with Nan suffered when she became anxious about her visions and tried to keep her daughter from seeing Perry to avoid danger, both confront their fears and their healthy, mutually supportive mother-daughter relationship is restored. Nan, rather than giving into her mother's fears and sacrificing her future life with Perry, is able to move forward into maturity and marriage. *Fantastic Summer,* then, is not just a straightforward narrative of maternal destruction. In her multilayered novel, Dorothy tells two stories about mothers, the restoration of a good mother and the destruction of a bad one, as well as stories about dysfunctional families and unhappy marriages and their effects on people's lives.

A decade after Dorothy heard the tale of murderous violence in a dysfunctional Dublin family, she creatively reimagined the Ball family story as one of the narrative strands in *Fantastic Summer.* Edward Ball is transformed into Perry Franks, also the son of an eminent Dublin doctor and an unstable mother who had separated before the mother's death. Dorothy wrote out Edward's homosexuality and lack of ambition, making Perry both heterosexual and a successful doctor. His late mother, Suzette, based partly on Vera Ball, had been erratic and cruel, with a particular animus towards Perry and his father, just as Vera had been especially hostile towards her son Edward and fought with him incessantly. Suzette ultimately left her husband and son to live in the south of France, where she died of food poisoning. Vera, rather than being a victim of food poisoning, had, according to Edward, tried to poison her husband.[13] Suzette continues to blight

11 Ibid., 278.          12 Ibid., 278.
13 Ibid., 101; Richard Cobb, *A Classical Education* (London: Chatto and Windus, 1985), 83.

the lives of the other characters after her death. Barnard, an idealized version of Dr Charles Ball, is emotionally drained by his difficult marriage, Perry struggles with anger and a quick temper, and Virgilia is unable to forget Suzette's violence. Vera Ball may have believed she had psychic powers. When she saw her estranged husband months before her death, she told him she envisioned something tragic happening, and hoped Edward would not be involved. At the time, Dr Ball thought she was being paranoid.[14] In *Fantastic Summer*, the character with psychic powers is partly based on Dorothy, rather than on Vera, and she has a vision of Perry taking part in murderous violence.

*Fantastic Summer*, unlike the story of the Ball family, has a happy ending. Dorothy may have been signalling her empathy for Edward, and her wish to nurture him and put his life to rights, by having Virgilia become Perry's mother-in-law. Perry, unlike Edward Ball, is ultimately able to control his anger, get married, experience professional success, and overcome the trauma of his relationship with his mother, whereas Edward, to Dorothy's dismay, was unable to do any of those things. Vera, unlike Suzette, was violently disposed of by her axe-wielding son, rather than disarmed through ridicule. Her disturbed son was institutionalized, spending years in the Dundrum Criminal Lunatic Asylum, "where some of the inmates [were] more dangerous than anything you'd find in Soledad or San Quentin."[15] When Dorothy returned from England, she was able to visit Edward again, as the asylum was a short distance from Creevagh. She successfully appealed to the authorities for his early release, as she had some influence with Éamon de Valera and the Fianna Fáil government, and Edward left the asylum in 1949 after being incarcerated for thirteen years. He moved to England shortly afterwards, living there for the rest of his life. Dorothy may have been an intellectual influence; when Edward met up with an old friend years later, "it was clear that, in the intervening years, he had read extensively in Anglo-Irish history."[16]

14 While Barnard is depicted as an innocent, long-suffering victim of Suzette and a devoted father to Perry in *Fantastic Summer*, Charles Ball was more complex, and had married Vera for her money. Cobb, *A Classical Education*, 37–8, 152. See also *Irish Press*, 23 May 1936, 8.

15 Joe Ambrose, *Too Much Too Soon* (London: Pulp Books, 2000), 132. In this novel, a Dublin journalist-historian visits a friend incarcerated in Dundrum.

16 Cobb, *A Classical Education*, 109, 151.

The Ball family tragedy resonated with Dorothy's own experience of family, which was why she found Edward Ball compelling. During her visits to the asylum over the years, Edward, who could be manipulative, seems to have won her sympathy with his disarming manner and stories about his childhood and adolescence with an erratic and abusive mother. Just as Vera Ball and Minnie Macardle bore some resemblance to one another, Edward's life ran parallel with Dorothy's in some respects. Besides coping with the separation of their parents and difficult relationships with unstable mothers, both found solace in the theatre. Dorothy feared the loss of her freedom and incarceration in institutions, whether in hospitals or convalescent homes. Like Virgilia, who developed concerns about her mental stability and consulted a psychiatrist, Dorothy appeared to worry about the possible decline of her mental stability later in life. Dorothy had spent time in prison, and Edward was confined to a criminal lunatic asylum, although both were released due to the intervention of influential people. Although she and Minnie were not especially fond of one another's company, Dorothy refrained from matricide, waiting until her mother was dead to achieve some release through repeated maternal destruction in her novels. Edward found release by succumbing to his violent fantasies.

*Fantastic Summer* reached transatlantic audiences. It made less of an impact than *The Uninvited*, as the novel's "invocation of extrasensory perception was not nearly as effective a heightening-device as a full-blooded haunting."[17] Dorothy was still involved with the Society for Psychical Research, and read case studies on ESP compiled by the Society. A *Times Literary Supplement* reviewer praised Dorothy's "sure feeling for Anglo-Irish ways and talk," as well as her plot construction, but felt the happy ending jarred with the book's darker undertones.[18] Dorothy's close friend, children's book author Patricia Lynch, thought the best part of *Fantastic Summer* was Dorothy's evocation of the Glencree setting in all its beguiling beauty, dramatically juxtaposed with the dark places in Virgilia's mind. Dorothy knew the Wicklow mountains well, having stayed in Glenmalure many times.[19]

17  Brian Stableford, "Dorothy Macardle," in David Pringle, ed., *St James Guide to Horror, Ghost, and Gothic Writers* (Detroit: St James Press, 1998), 382. An American edition, entitled *The Unforeseen*, was published by Doubleday in 1946.

18  W.R. LeFanu, review of *Fantastic Summer* by Dorothy Macardle, *Times Literary Supplement*, 15 June 1946, 281.

19  Patricia Lynch, review of *Fantastic Summer* by Dorothy Macardle, *Dublin*

A subplot in *Fantastic Summer* involves a group of itinerant tinkers (Travellers) camping in the glen. Virgilia foresees harm befalling a Traveller boy named Timeen, the son of a formidable woman named Sal Vaughan. Timeen has escaped back to the Vaughan clan from a reformatory, and is mistreated by his mother's new husband.[20] After he becomes acquainted with Virgilia, she has a vision of Timeen lying dead under a bridge, having drowned in the river on a rainy night.[21] Complications ensue when she entreats the Travellers to leave the glen earlier than they had planned to avoid danger to the child, and Sal curses Virgilia.[22] In the end, Virgilia arranges for Timeen to board with a local farming family, rather than stay with the Travellers or return to a reform school.[23]

The novel reflects Dorothy's concern about the fate of homeless, orphaned children in postwar Europe, as well as the treatment of children in care in Ireland in the 1940s. Virgilia worries about Timeen's well-being as well as his criminal potential, just as Dorothy was gravely concerned about destitute children turning to crime in Ireland and in war-ravaged Europe.[24] Virgilia, like Dorothy, dislikes institutionalization and reformatories and industrial schools; similarly, members of Irish women's groups who advocated for children in the 1930s and 1940s also maintained that probation for young offenders and the boarding out of neglected children with families were preferable to institutionalization.[25] As a reporter with the *Irish Press* in the 1930s, Dorothy had observed and written about the treatment of child offenders in the Dublin Children's Court, and knew that many were committed to institutions. Moreover, her friend Maud Gonne MacBride had written an exposé of the poor conditions in an industrial school in Glencree, Co. Wicklow, which was later shut down by the Fianna Fáil government, an incident mentioned in *Fantastic Summer*.[26] Dorothy later argued for legal adoption in

---

*Magazine*, vol. 21, no. 4 (October–December 1946), 59; RJD, NLI MS 32,582 (49), 4 August 1925.

20  Macardle, *Fantastic Summer*, 87–9, 126–7, 133.

21  Ibid., 136–7.

22  Ibid., 153–4.

23  Ibid., 133, 175–8, 193.

24  Ibid., 132–3.

25  RJD, NLI MS 32,582 (80), 3 November 1936; "Industrial Schools Inquiry," *Irish Press*, 23 October 1934, 3.

26  Maud Gonne MacBride, "The Industrial School Scandal," *An Phoblacht*, 4 September 1934; Macardle, *Fantastic Summer*, 108.

Ireland so that children would not have to spend their lives in orphanages and industrial schools. Although the abuses in Ireland's industrial school system were not widely known until the 1990s, there were individuals fifty years earlier, like Dorothy, who expressed reservations about Ireland's "architecture of containment."[27]

Dorothy's portrayal of Gypsies and Travellers in *Fantastic Summer* reflects a new understanding of itinerants that had been developing in Ireland for two decades, and marks her early intervention in the postwar debate about Travellers in Ireland.[28] The relationship between Travellers and settled people "deteriorated markedly after the Second World War when Travellers were defined by the majority community as a public problem."[29] In the 1920s and 1930s, government policies regarding street trading, schooling, land use, and public housing had brought Travellers into increasing conflict with the authorities. Popular awareness of the Traveller presence increased in the 1940s. With overseas travel ruled out during World War II, the Irish increasingly turned towards camping vacations in rural Ireland, where they encountered Travellers at campsites. New attitudes about the importance of attractive landscapes for tourist consumption "further denigrated Travellers by rendering their encampments unsightly to the all-important tourist."[30] Dorothy's characters' enjoyment of the beauty of the glens of Wicklow is hampered by the presence of the itinerant "problem." Her depiction of a Traveller boy who has been committed to a reform school was at variance with social reality. Traveller children, rather than being committed to institutions like poor settled children, were generally ignored by the authorities when they broke laws regarding begging and school attendance.[31] The Travellers may also have reminded Dorothy of the

27 James M. Smith, "Ireland's Architecture of Containment: Contemporary Narratives of the Nation State" (PhD Dissertation, Boston College, 1999).
28 In *Fantastic Summer*, the Vaughans, who have a Welsh surname, may be Anglo-Romanies, or Gypsies from Britain, rather than Irish Travellers. There were Gypsies living in Dublin, including a few families on Gardiner Street in the 1930s. See Aoife Bhreatnach, *Becoming Conspicuous: Irish Travellers, Society, and the State, 1922–1970* (Dublin: University College Dublin Press, 2006), 16–17. Dorothy could have encountered these families when visiting her friend Linda Kearns, who lived nearby on Gardiner Place, as well as seeing Gypsies and Travellers in Wicklow and other rural areas.
29 Bhreatnach, *Becoming Conspicuous,* 141.
30 Ibid., 60.
31 Ibid., 80–3.

homeless refugees she encountered in postwar Europe, an unfortunate but potentially destabilizing element in society. By the summer of 1946, there were impoverished refugees in Glencree, as German children were brought to a Red Cross centre there before being placed with Irish foster families.[32]

*Fantastic Summer*, then, is important for showing Dorothy's continuing interest in the supernatural and in problematic marriages and parent-child relationships. Once again, she tried to erase the baleful memory of a dreadful mother. The novel demonstrates her engagement, in the postwar period, with issues of importance to Irish women's groups and policymakers, such as juvenile delinquency and the institutionalization of children. The novel also explored the role of Travellers in Irish society, which became an area of heightened concern to Irish policymakers from the 1940s onwards.

Dorothy began researching and writing her second work of contemporary history, a book on the children of postwar Europe, in 1945. She wrote to the editor of the *Manchester Guardian* for help, asking if he would commission some articles on Czechoslovakia so that she could get a visa and travel there as a journalist.[33] The editor responded that he was familiar with her "excellent book," *The Irish Republic*, and regretted that he could not commission articles on Czechoslovakia from a freelancer, restrictions on the size of newspapers being what they were. He suggested trying to obtain a visa through a relief organization.[34] Dorothy appears to have followed his advice, and she submitted the manuscript for publication in December 1948. *Children of Europe*[35] stands out as a significant early contribution to the social history of World War II and its immediate aftermath. Covering themes such as children and war, the Holocaust, humanitarianism, psychology, collaboration and resistance, and liberal internationalism, the book represents Dorothy's last major

---

32  Cathy Molohan, *Germany and Ireland 1945–1955: Two Nations' Friendship* (Dublin: Irish Academic Press, 1999), 56–7.

33  Dorothy Macardle to the Editor of the *Manchester Guardian*, John Rylands Library, 24 November 1945.

34  Editor of the *Manchester Guardian* to Dorothy Macardle, John Rylands Library, 29 November 1945.

35  Dorothy Macardle, *Children of Europe, A Study of the Children of Liberated Countries: Their War-Time Experiences, Their Reactions, and Their Needs, With a Note on Germany* (London: Victor Gollancz, Ltd., 1949; reprint ed., Boston: Beacon Press, 1951). All of the following references are to the 1951 edition.

achievement in the areas of investigative journalism, contemporary history, and international humanitarianism.

Dorothy's personal history of humanitarianism and concern for children at both the national and international level extended back to her involvement in the White Cross during Ireland's War of Independence, and continued through the 1930s when she reported on the League of Nations in Geneva. The well-known children's welfare organization, the Save the Children International Union, was headquartered in Geneva, and the League of Nations also had social sections addressing child welfare. Thus, Dorothy, as a journalist, made professional contacts with children's advocates from many different countries. She made connections with refugees, including refugee children, in London during World War II. Her interest in child psychology dated back to her training as a teacher, and she kept up with new developments in psychology and education. Thus, by 1945 she was well-equipped to write a full-length study on the experiences and needs of children in war-devastated Europe.

Dorothy, now fifty-seven, travelled throughout Europe to meet with leaders of child welfare organizations in the spring of 1946. She conducted research in France, the Low Countries, Czechoslovakia and Switzerland. She interviewed government officials in the Health and Education and Social Welfare ministries in these countries, as well as physicians, educators, and child psychologists. Dorothy, who had spent much time in Geneva in the late 1930s, returned to Switzerland in 1946 to meet with International Red Cross officials, as well as with International Union for Child Welfare staff members. Now that the League of Nations had been succeeded by the United Nations, its humanitarian and social welfare sections, which had interested Dorothy in the 1930s, were replaced by UN organizations such as UNICEF, the United Nations International Children's Emergency Fund, which she strongly supported.[36] She mentioned the work of Catholic and other religious organizations involved in relief work, but focused more on secular, internationalist relief organizations. She can therefore be located in the tradition of secular Irish humanitarians and human rights proponents, such as Roger Casement and Alice Stopford Green,[37] while also anticipating later Irish support for

36 Dorothy Macardle, *Children of Europe* (Boston: Beacon Press, 1951), 15–16, 301.
37 For recent work on Green that discusses her humanitarianism and work with

international relief efforts carried out by UNICEF and secular
humanitarian non-governmental organizations. Dorothy was not the
only Irish humanitarian involved in relief efforts in postwar Europe.
Another prominent figure was Robert Collis, a pediatrician from
Dublin, who visited the Belsen concentration camp in Germany and
adopted two children he encountered there.[38] Dorothy's sources also
reveal that many women were deeply involved in postwar relief work
in Europe, just as there had been many women involved in interwar-
era humanitarianism. One of her counterparts, the Norwegian
feminist historian Mimi Sverdrup Lunden, also drew attention to the
plight of children in postwar Europe by writing a book similar to
*Children of Europe*, ironically titled *The Children's Century* (1948).[39]

Dorothy began *Children of Europe* by considering the ideological
environment of Nazi Germany and its impact on children. She felt
that inherent German "racial" qualities, the nature of the German
family, the political failures of the Weimar government, and the use
of the mass media and schools to bombard people with propaganda
had all combined to make the majority of Germans well-disposed
towards Nazism. Scouting and military training under Nazi leaders
held an added appeal for children and adolescents, who were easily
indoctrinated. German youth had a weak grasp of alternative
ideologies to counteract Nazism, as the Weimar government had not
pushed indoctrination in the schools; it had been "caught in that
dilemma which forbids liberalism to take drastic measures for its own
defence."[40] This foreshadowed Dorothy's response to the Cold War,
when she worried about the fate of liberal democracy in Western
Europe in light of the threat posed by Communism.

The first section of *Children of Europe* covers the fate of
Czechoslovakia, Poland, Greece, and Yugoslavia under Nazi occupation, as well as the fate of European Jews. Dorothy was most

Casement in human rights advocacy, see Nadia Clare Smith, *A 'Manly Study'?
Irish Women Historians, 1868–1949* (Basingstoke: Palgrave Macmillan, 2006),
37–60; Angus Mitchell, "Alice Stopford Green and the Origins of the African
Society," *History Ireland*, vol. 14, no. 4 (July–August 2006), 19–24.

38 Macardle, *Children of Europe*, 241; Alicia McAuley, "Bob Collis: 'the Irish
Schindler,'" *History Ireland*, vol. 14, no. 6 (November/December 2006), 8–9;
Margaret Ó hÓgartaigh, *Kathleen Lynn: Irishwoman, Patriot, Doctor* (Dublin:
Irish Academic Press, 2006) 131–2.

39 Ida Blom, "Women in Danish and Norwegian Historiography, c. 1900–c. 1960,"
*Storia della Storiografia*, vol. 46 (2004), 144.

40 Macardle, 30.

familiar with Czechoslovakia. She felt that this central European republic during the interwar period was almost an ideal society, commending Czechoslovakia's democratic politics, religious toleration, and liberal nationalism. She discussed the role of students and teachers in Czechoslovakia and Poland in resisting the Nazis.[41] Dorothy characterized the Nazi treatment of the Poles, Christians as well as Jews, as genocidal.[42] Overall, her treatment of the Poles' records under Nazi occupation contrasts sharply with late-twentieth century accounts, which tended to portray Poles as anti-Semitic bystanders or active Nazi collaborators, focusing less on Polish victimization and resistance.[43] Dorothy also discussed the Balkans, highlighting the work of international relief groups helping children in Greece, and the role of child partisans in the Resistance in Yugoslavia.[44]

The systematic extermination of over one million Jewish children in death camps, Dorothy stated, was "the most coldly vicious proceeding that has ever emanated from human brains." An atrocity unique in history, it could not be attributed to "fear or provocation or uncontrollable passion."[45] Thus, her discussion foreshadowed the theme of uniqueness that became prominent in late twentieth-century discussions of the Holocaust.[46] She traced the history of the Nazi persecution of the Jews, culminating in the Final Solution, and highlighted the experience of children in extermination camps.[47]

The second part of the book covers the Nazi occupation of Norway and Denmark, the Low Countries, and France. Dorothy wrote that in Norway and Denmark, most of the population, including children, passively resisted the Nazis. Turning to the Low Countries,[48] the Netherlands, Belgium, and Luxembourg, she high-

41 Macardle, 39–40, 49, 77.
42 Macardle, 65. She had read Raphael Lemkin's work on genocide. For Lemkin, see Peter Novick, *The Holocaust in American Life* (Boston: Houghton Mifflin, 1999), 100–101.
43 Novick, 222–3.
44 Macardle, 96, 102–3.
45 Macardle, 108.
46 Novick, 15, 195–8.
47 Macardle, 109–14.
48 For a recent work on the Netherlands, Belgium, and France during and after World War II, see Pieter Lagrou, *The Legacy of Nazi Occupation: Patriotic Memory and National Recovery in Western Europe, 1945–1965* (Cambridge: Cambridge University Press, 2000). See also N. David J. Barnouw, "Dutch Exiles in London," in Martin Conway and Jose Gotovitch, eds., *Europe in Exile: European Exile Communities in Britain 1940–45* (New York: Bergahn Books, 2001), 229–46.

lighted the anti-Nazi resistance and the postwar problems of children. Few children were successfully indoctrinated by Nazi teachers or attracted to the Hitler Youth, but the stresses of war took their toll on children's behaviour. Dorothy was pleased that in Belgium and Luxembourg, some schools stressed progressive education after the war to promote democratic thought.[49] In her discussion of France, Dorothy condemned the Vichy government and collaborators, but presented the majority of the French people as resisting the Nazis. She also praised the French effort to save Jews.[50]

The last section of the book concentrates on the massive deprivation and trauma with which children were contending in postwar Europe, and on efforts to help them. Mental health professionals, international aid organizations, and progressive educators all had a role to play. Dorothy interviewed child psychologists about the psychological responses of children to the trauma of war, and about methods of treatment.[51] She discussed the work of international relief groups such as Save the Children, the Red Cross, and UNICEF.[52] Lastly, she described new educational practices in schools designed to inculcate a democratic spirit in students, as well as group homes for war orphans where the children practised some self-government.[53]

While Dorothy adopted an inclusive approach by surveying the experience of children in most European countries during World War II, there are, nevertheless, certain silences and exclusions in her book. There is no discussion of the European Gypsies, who were targeted by the Nazis and sent to Auschwitz and other death camps. Over two hundred thousand Gypsies were killed; some who had managed to evade death joined anti-Nazi resistance movements. However, Dorothy did not tell their stories, although she noted that "to Jewish and Gypsy and mentally defective children a process of elimination was to be applied" by the Nazis.[54] There may have been gaps in the

---

49  Macardle, 160–80.
50  Macardle, 181–95. Later historians discussed the "Gaullist myth of a nation of resisters" promoted after the war, which "gloss[ed] over the awkward reality of how few French men and women were involved in Resistance." Hanna Diamond, *Women and the Second World War in France* (New York: Pearson, 1999), 183–4.
51  Macardle, 226, 252–9.
52  Macardle, 220–1, 301–3.
53  Macardle, 210–11, 272–84, 306–12.
54  Macardle, 12. For Gypsy children, see Sybil Milton, "Non-Jewish Children in the Camps," in Michael Berenbaum, ed., *A Mosaic of Victims* (New York: New York University Press, 1990), 150–60. Historians estimate that "by 1945, the

records of international aid organizations in regard to Gypsies, depriving Dorothy of evidence.[55]

Overall, *Children of Europe* is the work of a liberal internationalist and humanitarian. Like many of the experts she interviewed for the book, Dorothy had come from a background of interwar-era humanitarianism centered on the League of Nation's social and health sections, and related independent organizations such as Save the Children. Now that the United Nations had superseded the League of Nations, Dorothy shifted her support to new organizations such as UNESCO and UNICEF. UNICEF, which impartially aided children in need, was funded by governments and individuals. Its campaign to feed malnourished children in postwar Europe, Dorothy maintained, was one "to which no human being can take exception ... if UNICEF succeeds in its aims the child welfare work of the whole civilized world will become a co-operative enterprise."[56] She included the text of the League of Nations' Declaration of the Rights of the Child, which she and other children's advocates hoped the UN would adopt. A modified version of the Declaration was adopted by the UN in 1959.[57]

*Children of Europe* received a favourable critical response. It was reviewed in Ireland by Dorothy's friend R.M. Fox, a progressive journalist and writer. He was horrified by the Nazi program to brutalize children, but was inspired by Dorothy's account of the Norwegian teachers' resistance to the Nazis. Fox was most struck by "the widespread suffering which may be caused by [ordinary] people

Nazis had murdered at least 220,000 of the estimated 700,000 European Gypsies." Konnilyn Feig, "Non-Jewish Victims in the Concentration Camps," in Berenbaum, *A Mosaic of Victims*, 68.

55 She noted that the reports of many organizations were still incomplete and "quantitative data [was] almost entirely lacking." Macardle, *Children of Europe*, 12.

56 Macardle, 301–3. For more on international aid organizations between the 1920s and 1940s, see Dominique Marshall, "Humanitarian Sympathy for Children in Times of War and the History of Children's Rights, 1919–1959," in James Marten, ed., *Children and War: A Historical Anthology* (New York: New York University Press, 2002), 184–99; and Patricia T. Rooke and Rudy L. Schnell, " 'Uncramping Child Life': International Children's Organizations, 1914–1939," in Paul Weindling, ed., *International Health Organizations and Movements, 1918–1939* (Cambridge: Cambridge University Press, 1995), 176–202. For UNICEF, see Maggie Black, *Children First: The Story of UNICEF, Past and Present* (Oxford: Oxford University Press, 1996).

57 Macardle, *Children of Europe*, 313; Marshall, "Humanitarian Sympathy for Children in Times of War," 196.

lacking the moral courage to make a stand against evil,"[58] anticipating the later twentieth-century Holocaust discourse about bystanders who chose to remain silent.[59] Gwendolen Freeman reviewed the book in the *Times Literary Supplement*. While she found the relentless recounting of Nazi atrocities numbing, she was heartened by stories of resilience and compassion, as well as by knowing that individuals could make a difference by contributing to aid organizations and sponsoring needy children.[60]

*Children of Europe* was written both to document children's wartime experience for future researchers, and to urge ordinary people to help by contributing to international aid organizations, particularly UNICEF. Prior to the book's publication, Dorothy gave broadcasts on the plight of children in postwar Europe, illustrating her belief in the need to raise awareness of the situation as soon as possible. In the autumn of 1946, she planned three talks on the BBC: "The Children in Hiding," "The Unclaimed Child," and "Lost and Found."[61] She gave a broadcast on Radio Éireann on "Missing Children of Europe" in 1947.[62] *Children of Europe* has also been used as a resource by later historians.[63]

The 1940s were an extremely productive decade for Dorothy. Despite the death and destruction surrounding her in wartime London, she managed to combine a demanding writing schedule, humanitarian work, and radio journalism. Although she was in her late fifties and in indifferent health, she undertook a gruelling research trip through war-devastated European countries to bear witness to the war's disastrous toll on children.

58 R.M. Fox, review of *Children of Europe* by Dorothy Macardle, *Dublin Magazine*, vol. 25, no.2 (April-June 1950), 58–9.
59 Novick, 179, 245, 255.
60 Gwendolen Freeman, review of *Children of Europe* by Dorothy Macardle, *Times Literary Supplement*, 13 January 1950, 22.
61 Dorothy Macardle to Mr. MacAlpine, Dorothy Macardle File, BBC WAC, 14 August 1946, 20 September 1946.
62 Her talk was printed in the Alexandra College Magazine. Dorothy Macardle, "Missing Children of Europe," *Alexandra College Magazine*, vol. 10 (June 1947), 3–6.
63 Mark Wyman, *DPs: Europe's Displaced Persons, 1945–1951* (1989; Cornell University Press, 1998). Wyman turned to *Children of Europe* for his chapter on displaced children.

# CHAPTER EIGHT

# Dublin in the 1950s

IRELAND OFFICIALLY BECAME a republic in April 1949, a month after Dorothy's sixtieth birthday. She spent most of the 1950s in Ireland. Despite her indifferent health and feelings of alienation as an aging revolutionary whose generation was being surpassed by the next one, she remained socially and politically engaged, and continued to travel and write. As part of a circle of outspoken liberal political activists, she helped pave the way for the social changes of the 1960s and a more open, less authoritarian political and cultural climate.

Ireland in the 1950s was not entirely in keeping with Dorothy's liberal, secular, republican ideals, and the polarized Cold War world challenged her liberal internationalism. Fianna Fáil had been replaced in 1948 by a coalition government of Fine Gael and Clann na Poblachta, a progressive new party, but returned to power from 1951 to 1954, and again in 1957. Ireland faced high unemployment and emigration throughout the decade, and progressives like Dorothy were critical of the political influence of the Catholic Church, and of policies such as censorship. As a western European country, Ireland was also affected by the postwar tensions between communism and capitalism, totalitarianism and democracy, and the potential threats posed by communism to western democracies in the age of the Cold War. Dorothy strenuously denounced the Soviet Union and communism, and was particularly critical of the communist takeover of Czechoslovakia, a country she had always admired for its liberal democracy.[1] She was unenthusiastic about nuclear disarmament,[2] believing that in the

1 RJD, NLI MS 32,582 (133), 26 March 1949.
2 RJD, NLI MS 32,582 (161), 7 February 1958.

postwar world, the Soviets had replaced the Nazis as the most dangerous threat to the West, and that the USSR could be deterred by nuclear weapons. Dorothy also had unfocused notions about evil that seemed to stand apart from Cold War politics. She thought it was loathsome for people to have to live in dread of nuclear war, and that it now "seem[ed] as if Anti-Christ is in power on Earth."[3]

The Irish Association of Civil Liberties, founded in 1948, played a central role in promoting individual rights in Ireland in the 1950s. Dorothy was a founding member, and became actively involved in many of the association's campaigns. The group had its roots in the short-lived Society for Intellectual Freedom, which had fought censorship in the early 1940s. Other members of the Civil Liberties Association included solicitor Christopher Gore-Grimes, politicians James Douglas and Owen Sheehy Skeffington, feminists Rosamond Jacob and Hilda Tweedy, the writer Seán Ó Faoláin, and Michael Yeats, the son of W.B. Yeats. The group, centered in Dublin, consisted mainly of liberals and a few leftists, and older activists like Dorothy and Rosamond Jacob mixed with younger progressives, such as Owen Sheehy Skeffington, the son of the late feminist leader Hanna Sheehy Skeffington. A participant suggested that one of the Association's objectives should be to "combat all totalitarianisms, Communist or Fascist – this got a majority, but Seán Ó Faoláin got 'so far as consonant with individual liberty' stuck on."[4] The Civil Liberties Association brought in new members within a short period, including academics such as Trinity College historian T.W. Moody and UCD literature professor Roger McHugh.[5]

The Civil Liberties Association campaigned for legal adoption in Ireland in the early 1950s, and Dorothy added her voice to the campaign. She was impatient with government foot-dragging on legislation, and challenged official reasons given for not legalizing adoption. She believed that adoption was opposed by people who hoped to inherit from childless relatives, as well as by those who wished to punish illegitimate children for their parents' sexual behaviour, and that they were being disingenuous when they claimed they opposed adoption because a child could be adopted by parents of a different religion. Dorothy noted that safeguards could be built

3 Dorothy Macardle to Kathleen O'Connell, UCDA P155/127(6), n.d. [late 1940s].
4 RJD, NLI MS 32,582 (127), 22 March 1948.
5 RJD, NLI MS 32,582 (128), 12 May 1948.

6. Dorothy Macardle, 1952.
(Source: Proinnsios
Ó Duigneáin, *Linda Kearns:
A Revolutionary Irish
Woman*, Drumlin
Publications, 2002. Used with
the author's permission)

into adoption legislation; in the meantime, since adoption was unregulated, a child could indeed be adopted by people of a different religion. She concluded that adoption would one day be legalized; it was only a matter of when, as "we are not so backward and callous a people that we will continue indefinitely to incarcerate children in institutions while there are people eager to give them family life."[6] Adoption was legalized in 1952, due more to negative publicity surrounding unregulated adoptions than to a popular campaign.[7]

Between 1952 and 1954, a few members of the Civil Liberties Association expressed interest in investigating the Magdalen asylums, which were run by nuns.[8] Originally established for prostitutes in the eighteenth century, Magdalen asylums, by the twentieth century, incarcerated "wayward girls," including unmarried mothers and victims

6 Dorothy Macardle, letter, *Irish Times*, 16 October 1950, 5.
7 Mike Milotte, *Banished Babies* (Dublin: New Island Books, 1997).
8 There were also a few Protestant asylums, including one on Leeson Street in Dublin that lasted until the 1950s. See *Thom's Directory* (Dublin, 1951).

of sexual assault. Some were institutionalized for life, working in laundries attached to the asylums. The Magdalen asylums were secretive institutions with no state funding or legal standing, but the inmates were unaware of their rights, and needed outside intervention for release. The laundries were gradually phased out between the 1970s and 1990s. As was the case with industrial schools, the abuses and deprivations experienced by the inmates were not widely known until the 1990s.[9]

The subject of investigating conditions in the Magdalen laundries was first raised at a Civil Liberties meeting in 1952. Seán Ó Faoláin, who was chairing the meeting, suddenly became evasive, but Dorothy's friend Rosamond Jacob pointed out that the Association had formed a visiting committee to investigate conditions in the Dundrum Criminal Lunatic Asylum. Ó Faoláin then agreed that a subcommittee should be put together.[10] A few months later, it was announced at a Civil Liberties meeting that the Joint Committee of Women's Societies and Social Workers planned to investigate the Magdalen asylums. One man felt it was an affront to the nuns, revealing how controversial it was to question institutions run by religious orders in Ireland at the time, especially ones associated with the containment of female sexuality.[11] When the Civil Liberties Association met again in 1954, Jacob was put on a subcommittee to investigate the laundries, and Helen Chenevix Trench, a feminist and trade union activist, commented on "the lack of asylums for unmarried fathers and penitent males." The Association members were uncertain about whether they could visit an asylum, as they thought an appeal for help needed to be made to them before they could ask for more information.[12]

Dorothy's views on the Magdalen asylums, as a member of the Civil Liberties Association, are undocumented. As someone with an interest in problematic female sexuality, prisoners, and Gothic institutions that repressed and confined women,[13] an investigation of

9  James M. Smith, "The Politics of Sexual Knowledge: the Origins of Ireland's Containment Culture and the Carrigan Report (1931)," *Journal of the History of Sexuality*, vol. 13, no. 2 (April 2004), 208–33; Maria Luddy, review of *Do Penance or Perish: A Study of the Magdalen Asylums in Ireland* by Frances Finnegan, *American Historical Review* 110:2 (April 2005).
10  RJD, NLI MS 32,582 (145), 17 November 1952.
11  RJD, NLI MS 32,582 (146), 12 March 1953.
12  RJD, NLI MS 32,582 (150), 18 May 1954, 10 June 1954.
13  For a discussion of Magdalen asylums as Gothic institutions, see Elizabeth Butler

a Magdalen asylum, and the possibility of eventually liberating the female inmates, should surely have intrigued her. A former inmate of a women's prison, she disliked institutionalization and had spoken out against industrial schools. However, Dorothy may have found the asylums and their inmates too distasteful, as well as controversial, for public discussion. Her notions of class, gender, and sexuality may have been placed ahead of her libertarianism and feminism in this case. Instead of viewing the Magdalens as disempowered women denied their civil rights, Dorothy may have perceived them as lower-class sexual transgressors who could have a corrupting influence on society if they were released, and whose rights, therefore, did not need to be vigorously defended by civil libertarians. Many Irish feminists of Dorothy's generation favoured the institutionalization of girls perceived as sexual transgressors, and were not especially concerned about the denial of individual rights that this entailed.[14]

The campaign to commute the death sentence of Mary Ann Cadden was a high profile cause taken up by the Civil Liberties Association from late 1956 to early 1957. Cadden was a nurse who had performed an illegal abortion on Helen O'Reilly, a married woman and mother of several children whose husband was working in Nigeria. O'Reilly subsequently died, and her body was found on Hume Street, near St Stephen's Green. The elderly Cadden was erratic and incoherent. The Civil Liberties Association, which now included academic historians T.W. Moody and T.D. Williams among its vice presidents, argued that she should be sentenced to life imprisonment, and circulated a petition to be signed. The government commuted Cadden's sentence.[15]

Two of Dorothy's oldest friends, Linda Kearns MacWhinney and Maud Gonne MacBride, died in the 1950s. Linda, Dorothy's closest friend and a long-term political ally, died in June 1951. Like Dorothy, she had been an original member of the Fianna Fáil executive, and had briefly served in the Senate before returning to her private nursing practice. After separating from her husband, Charles MacWhinney, a

Cullingford, "Our Nuns are Not a Nation," *Éire-Ireland*, 41:1&2, Spring/Summer 2006.

14  James M. Smith, "The Politics of Sexual Knowledge," 208–33.

15  For details on the Cadden case, see NAI, TAOIS/s16116. See also Sandra McAvoy, "Before Cadden: Abortion in Mid-Twentieth Century Ireland," in Dermot Keogh, Finbarr O'Shea, and Carmel Quinlan (eds.), *The Lost Decade: Ireland in the 1950s* (Cork: Mercier Press, 2004), 147–63.

Protestant republican from Northern Ireland, Linda lived with their daughter Ann in Dublin, and they often visited Dorothy. After Linda's death, Dorothy remained close to Ann, her god-daughter.[16] Maud Gonne MacBride, who died in April 1953, had been influential in Dorothy's life decades earlier, when she helped bring her into the republican fold, and they had worked together for years as allies in the White Cross and the Women's Prisoners Defence League. Maud's son, Seán MacBride, whom Dorothy had known since his youth, was a founding member of Clann na Poblachta and an influential political figure in Ireland from the 1950s through the 1980s.

Friends noticed that Dorothy seemed to get more eccentric as she got older. She had always been interested in the supernatural, and became more interested in witchcraft in her last years. One day, when two women came to visit Dorothy at Benedin, her new house in Howth, she told them that an invisible familiar, in the form of a little girl, followed her about. Folk traditions about witches held that they were accompanied by familiars in various guises, usually black cats. Dorothy further informed her guests that if they moved a string around the house and felt a magnetic pull, it would indicate the presence of a ghost as well as their own psychic powers. When the visitors tried this, one felt nothing, but the other felt a slight pull.[17]

While Dorothy enjoyed her life in Dublin in the 1950s, with its full round of activities and socializing with friends, she developed a number of concerns as she grew older. As a member of an older, revolutionary generation in Ireland, she felt increasingly unappreciated, and believed that younger Irish people had forgotten the accomplishments of their predecessors. Her health had always been a concern, and she grew more fragile in her sixties. As she suffered from lung trouble, she spent winters abroad in warmer, drier climates. Her last novel hints that as she grew older, she may have become concerned about the gradual onset of mental instability, possibly leading to institutionalization and loss of her freedom.

Dorothy continued to travel in the 1950s, and spent many winters in the south of France. She stayed in the village of Roquebrune in 1952 and 1953, where she wrote *Dark Enchantment*, a "light novel"

---

16  Proinnsios Ó Duigneáin, *Linda Kearns: A Revolutionary Irish Woman* (Nure, Co. Leitrim: Drumlin Publications, 2002); Dorothy Macardle, "Portrait of a Happy Warrior," *Irish Press*, 11 June 1952, 4.
17  Eunan O'Halpin to author, 25 February 2004.

set in contemporary Provence and dealing with witchcraft.[18] The novel's young British heroine, Juliet Cunningham, works at an inn run by René Loubier, a former member of the French Resistance, and his wife, Martine, in the village of St Jacques.[19] Juliet's parents are divorced, and she feels abandoned by her mother, who has left for South America. She learns of the village's fear and hatred of Terka, a one-eyed Gypsy woman and reputed witch, who had been romantically involved with René Loubier during World War II when both were in the Resistance. Terka is blamed for causing a number of catastrophes through diabolical means, and particularly terrifies Martine. Local men, including René, plan to kill the suspected witch. Juliet, in the meantime, begins a relationship with Michael Faulkner, an Englishman visiting Provence, and they try to solve the mystery of whether or not Terka used supernatural means to cause misfortunes. Ultimately, Terka is confined to a mental institution, and Michael and Juliet plan to marry and leave Provence.

*Dark Enchantment* reflected a number of Dorothy's anxieties at the time, which she displaced onto Terka.[20] Like Dorothy, Terka was a former revolutionary who now felt alienated and unwanted. Those who reject her include men who had once been her comrades in the struggle, but were unable to cope with strong-willed, unconventional women in the postwar period. Terka is condemned by the local priest, just as Dorothy and other republicans were excommunicated in the Civil War. Dorothy apparently identified more with witches in her later years, claiming she had a familiar, and Terka is suspected of being a witch. Terka is shown to be mentally unstable, and is ultimately institutionalized, while Dorothy worried about her own health and stability and feared confinement and loss of freedom. Lastly, Terka is a childless single woman who had been sexually active in her youth, while Dorothy was a childless single woman who had experienced close relationships with other women, and both

18 Dorothy Macardle to Móirín Chevasse, MacSwiney Papers, UCDA P48c/182–3, 16 March 1953, 11 July 1953.

19 Dorothy Macardle, *Dark Enchantment* (Garden City, New York: Doubleday & Company, 1953), 21–80. The Loubiers were based on innkeepers Dorothy met in the south of France, who told stories about witches to their guests. Dorothy Macardle, "They Say It Happened," Broadcast Talk, RTÉ Written Archives, 31 October 1955.

20 I am indebted to Gerardine Meaney for discussing characterization in *Dark Enchantment* with me. Gerardine Meaney, conversation with author, 20 February 2006.

were, therefore, at odds with their societies, which extolled marriage and motherhood.

In Dorothy's novels, deviant women are destroyed or disempowered so that others can escape their haunting power and move on. Echoes of her conflict with her own mother were continually rehearsed and resolved in her later fiction. In *Dark Enchantment*, Terka, rather than an oppressive mother figure, fulfils the role of the dangerous, diabolical older woman who haunts younger women. Juliet is initially drawn to Terka through compassion, but later condemns her unreservedly.[21] Her walk through the woods to Terka's sinister-looking house, where she goes to have her fortune told,[22] represents an unsettling journey into the unconscious. In this female Gothic novel, a witch, rather than a ghost, functions as the manifestation of a young woman's fear of deviance, which must be confronted and repressed if she is to become a mature adult.[23] After a final confrontation and Terka's erasure, Juliet is ready to move forward successfully into adulthood, marriage and motherhood. The deviant outsider, Terka, is punished and incarcerated, while Juliet embraces marriage and acceptable femininity in the novel's conventional happy ending.

*Dark Enchantment* was not as widely reviewed as *Uneasy Freehold*, nor was it as much of a commercial success. Like Dorothy's other supernatural novels, it was first published in Britain by Peter Davies, and then in the United States by Doubleday. A *Dublin Magazine* critic praised Dorothy's evocation of setting, and commented that the novel raised intriguing questions about the power of evil and of a witch's curse. Juliet, however, did not seem English to the reviewer, as she was too curious about mysteries, and had a "questing soul."[24] A *New York Times* reviewer perceived *Dark Enchantment* as a nostalgic book about a vanished, prewar France, a "fairy-tale country of peasants, childlike innkeepers, gypsy witches, naïve lovers … superstitious, easily inflamed villagers and credulous women." She praised the descriptions of Provence and the novel's

21  *Dark Enchantment*, 302.
22  Ibid., 98–117.
23  For the conventions of the "female Gothic" genre, see Misha Kavka, "The Gothic On Screen," in Jerrold E. Hogle, ed., *The Cambridge Companion to Gothic Fiction* (New York: Cambridge University Press, 2002), 219–21.
24  "T.D.," review of *Dark Enchantment* by Dorothy Macardle, *Dublin Magazine*, vol. XXX, no. 3 (July–September 1954), 73–4.

escapist aspect, maintaining that the incidents "entertain but never seriously disturb us."[25] A reviewer for the *New York Herald Tribune* found Terka more compelling and intriguing than Juliet, and hoped Dorothy would write another book detailing Terka's story.[26]

In her Foreword, Dorothy claimed that while *Dark Enchantment* was a work of fiction, there was a factual basis behind some of the incidents and folk beliefs. Witchcraft conflict survived in France and elsewhere in Europe well into the middle decades of the twentieth century. *Dark Enchantment* was published just two years after the repeal of the 1736 Witchcraft Act in Britain, and the last court case dealing with an assault on a suspected witch in England occurred in 1947.[27] Witch conflicts took place in Continental Europe in the 1950s and 1960s, and tended to occur in small, relatively isolated, close-knit, rural communities, like the fictional village of St Jacques. However, modernization and more recent social conflicts could play a role in generating witchcraft panics. For example, "the rise of German witchcraft cases in the 1950s has been attributed to the influx of single women into village communities after the war," and in France in the 1960s, witchcraft accusations occurred in rural areas experiencing economic dislocation.[28]

Dorothy continued to keep in touch with friends at Alexandra College, and was invited to give a speech to a group of graduates in London in 1952. She now seemed to identify as Anglo-Irish, although she did not come from an Irish Protestant background. She lauded the Anglo-Irish as she reflected on political and social changes in Ireland and England in the last half-century. Dorothy believed that an ethos of noblesse oblige held a central place in the mentality of Alexandra College graduates, most of whom came from Irish Protestant backgrounds, though not all were as wealthy as the Macardles. She felt that the rise of the welfare state in postwar Britain had limited the ability of wealthy women to exercise power and

---

25 Evelyn Eaton, "The Dancing Daughter," review of *Dark Enchantment* by Dorothy Macardle, *New York Times*, Section VII, 4, 29 November 1953.
26 Shirley Barker, *New York Herald Tribune*, November 29, 1953, 8.
27 Owen Davies, *Witchcraft, Magic, and Culture, 1736–1951* (Manchester: Manchester University Press, 1999), 327.
28 Willem de Blecourt, "The Witch, Her Victim, the Unwitcher, and the Researcher: the Continued Existence of Traditional Witchcraft" in Bengt Ankarloo and Stuart Clark, eds., *Witchcraft and Magic in Europe in the Twentieth Century* (Philadelphia: University of Pennsylvania Press, 1999), 214.

influence by dispensing charity. In Ireland, Dorothy stated, elderly Anglo-Irish women were not highly valued, but she believed they nevertheless gave tirelessly of themselves in the service of others.[29]

Dorothy was still a republican. In April 1956, she was invited to give a radio talk on James Connolly and Patrick Pearse for the Thomas Davis lecture series. She maintained that the 1916 Rising and War of Independence were justified, and that Connolly and Pearse were admirable.[30] In the 1950s she looked back at promising figures in Irish nationalism who had died relatively young and had been unable to shape the new Ireland. She wished that more liberal, intellectual figures had lived longer. Late in life she professed anger that the government had no work for her "because she was unorthodox," and argued that literary censorship had killed the Irish literary revival.[31] It was interesting that Dorothy was asked to speak on the Thomas Davis lecture series, as the broadcasts were mainly given by younger, professional historians. The lectures were edited for publication by Conor Cruise O'Brien, a politician and historian, as well as the nephew of Dorothy's old friend Hanna Sheehy Skeffington.

The IRA began a border campaign in 1956 that lasted until 1962, though there were few casualties. Their main targets were police barracks just over the border in Northern Ireland. Dorothy had been a government supporter since Fianna Fáil came to power in the early 1930s, and opposed paramilitaries like the IRA trying to influence public policy through violence. While she personally opposed Partition, declaring that "a section of our territory is excluded from freedom and our fellow-nationalists in Ulster still suffer raids, arrest, and imprisonment without trial,"[32] she agreed with the Fianna Fáil view that Partition could be ended through peaceful political means. The Civil Liberties Association members were hardly IRA supporters, but some of the more libertarian members argued against repressive legislation, such as internment. Dorothy was not especially concerned with this policy. At a 1958 meeting in which internment was dis-

29 *Alexandra College Dublin Magazine*, vol. 11 (June 1952), 6–9.
30 Dorothy Macardle, "James Connolly and Patrick Pearse," in Conor Cruise O'Brien, ed., *The Shaping of Modern Ireland* (London: Routledge and Kegan Paul, 1960), 185–95.
31 L.C. LeFanu, *Alexandra College Dublin Magazine*, vol. 11 (December 1959).
32 Dorothy Macardle, "Without Fanfares, Some Reflections on the Republic of Éire," *The Commonweal*, 30 November 1945, 164.

cussed, Dorothy was "very anti the prisoners of course."[33] The only Irish prisoner who interested her in recent years, it seemed, was Edward Ball. When the Association had discussed Emergency laws still on the books in the late 1940s, Dorothy and "one or two other ardent Fianna Fáil admirers" objected to the word "tyrannical" being used to describe a Minister's power to imprison people indefinitely without trial.[34] Dorothy's anti-libertarian stance in this regard, at variance with her stance in the 1920s, probably stems from her belief, intensified after World War II, that democratic states like Ireland needed to take strong measures to defend themselves against challengers such as militant nationalists or totalitarians. She felt that this was a dilemma for all liberal democratic states, but left it at that.

The *Illustrated London News* published one of Dorothy's stories, "The Crystal Star," in 1956. During the past decade, she had become preoccupied with children turning to a life of crime and corruption, stemming from her experience as an investigative journalist in war-ravaged Europe, when she reported on children turning to crime for survival. She worried about a whole generation of juvenile delinquents growing up in postwar Europe. "The Crystal Star" centres on an earnest, naïve, self-absorbed Englishwoman named Judith who convalesces in an Austrian mountain village following her departure from a local sanatorium. Like Dorothy, who had also spent time in the mountains of Austria and Switzerland for health reasons, she suffers from lung trouble. She befriends Thérèse, a young girl who does odd jobs for her, and initially views Thérèse as angelic and innocent. When Judith discovers a pendant missing, however, she is nearly overcome with shock and grief, believing Thérèse has stolen the pendant. She wonders if she has exposed the girl to temptation and corruption by showing her an expensive piece of jewelry. Judith indirectly accuses Thérèse of stealing, and returns to England. She later learns she was mistaken and that the pendant was simply misplaced, but when she tries to make amends with Thérèse, her overtures are rebuffed, and the damage done to their friendship appears irreparable.[35]

33 RJD, NLI MS 32,582 (163), 25 June 1958.
34 RJD, NLI MS 32,582 (134), 3 May 1949.
35 Dorothy Macardle, "The Crystal Star," *Illustrated London News*, vol. 229, Christmas number, 9 November 1956.

Dorothy's love of theatre remained undiminished. She became interested in the rise of Dublin's Pike Theatre in the 1950s. The Pike, run by Carolyn Swift, produced challenging new works, including plays by Brendan Behan and Samuel Beckett. Dorothy took part in a discussion of Beckett's *Waiting for Godot* following a performance in February 1956, stating that the play was "an unbearable picture of human misery."[36] In April 1957, she attended the Shakespeare Festival in Stratford-on-Avon. She wrote to the BBC about giving a broadcast on the Festival, but nothing appears to have come of this.[37] Over the next year she spent time in Stratford researching and writing a study of Shakespeare aimed at a school-age readership.[38] Her book examined the political, cultural, and social history of Elizabethan England, and outlined the plots of the plays and discussed characterization.[39] In a way, things had come full circle. She had a lifelong love of Shakespeare, and some of her first efforts as a writer involved editing Shakespeare's plays for school textbooks.[40] Her final effort as a writer was also related to Shakespeare, and her last book, *Shakespeare, Man and Boy*, was published posthumously.

In late 1957, Dorothy was diagnosed with colon cancer.[41] Her condition worsened progressively over the next year. She was attended to by her god-daughter Ann MacWhinney Keating, but was eventually moved to Lourdes Hospital in Drogheda, Co. Louth, which was run by the Medical Missionaries of Mary. Éamon de Valera visited her in the hospital, and prayed for her return to Catholicism, but to no avail.[42] Dorothy regretted that she was unable to attend the Women Writers' Club silver jubilee at the Royal Hibernian Hotel in early December, where she was scheduled to preside at a dinner to honour Rosamond Jacob for her book *The Rebel's Wife*.[43] Dorothy wanted to spare her family the knowledge of the seriousness of her condition, so that they

36  Carolyn Swift, *Stage by Stage* (Dublin, 1985), 194–5.
37  Dorothy Macardle to the Director of Talks, Dorothy Macardle File, BBC Written Archives Centre, April 1957.
38  F.G. [Frank Gallagher], "An Appreciation," *Irish Press*, 24 December 1958, 5.
39  Dorothy Macardle, *Shakespeare, Man and Boy* (London: Faber, 1960). The book was edited for publication by George Bott, who wrote an introduction.
40  Peter Tremayne, "A Reflection of Ghosts," in Stephen Jones and Jo Fletcher, eds, *Gaslight and Ghosts* (London: Robinson, 1988), 88.
41  Dorothy Macardle, Death Certificate, General Record Office of Ireland.
42  Tim Pat Coogan, De Valera: *Long Fellow, Long Shadow* (London, 1995), 500.
43  "M.A.T.," *Dublin Evening Mail*, 26 November 1958.

could enjoy the Christmas season, but she died on December 23, 1958, at the age of sixty-nine.

The funeral was held the next day. The officiants were two Church of Ireland clergymen, Canon Johnston and Reverend McNutt.[44] The chief mourners were Dorothy's siblings and her Everard, Bevan, and Moore cousins. Éamon de Valera made an appearance. Ministers from the Fianna Fáil government who attended the funeral included Frank Aiken, Oscar Traynor and Seán MacEntee, whom she had known since her revolutionary days, Erskine Childers, the son of her beloved friend and mentor was also in attendance. Other friends and associates included Ann Keating, Frank and Cecilia Gallagher, Christopher Gore-Grimes from the Civil Liberties Association, and Madeline Ross of the Women Writers' Club. There was also an IRA presence in St Fintan's Cemetery in Howth that day, due to Dorothy's background. Dorothy's coffin, draped with the Irish flag, was "removed from the hearse and carried to the cemetery by members of the Four Courts Garrison, IRA (1922), who also formed a guard of honour."[45] Dorothy's headstone read "In Loving Memory of Dorothy Macardle, Born 7th March 1889, Died 23rd December 1958, Historian, Novelist, Lecturer, She Fought For Freedom."

Dorothy was able to leave her younger siblings well provided for, as her assets totalled more than nine thousand pounds. Her youngest brother Donald was the sole executor of her will. He received five hundred pounds and his sister's furniture and books, while Dorothy's jewellery was left to Donald's wife Enid. John Macardle received fifty pounds and some property. Mona Macardle received one hundred pounds and the residue of her sister's estate, but a codicil to the will revoked the residuary bequest from Mona and bequeathed it to Donald, who would decide on an annuity for Mona. Smaller sums were left to her cousins, friends such as Nora Connolly O'Brien, her god-daughter Ann MacWhinney Keating, the trustees of the Alexandra College Guild House, and the Medical Missionaries of Mary in Drogheda, County Louth. Éamon de Valera's son Terry was made the copyright holder of *The Irish Republic*.[46]

44 Thomas Johnston was the Rector of Raheny, the editor of the *Church of Ireland Monthly*, and an author of works on Church of Ireland history. Alfred Thompson McNutt of St Jude's Church of Ireland, Kilmainham, read the prayers in Irish.
45 "Funeral of Miss Dorothy Macardle," *Irish Press*, 25–27 December 1958, 7.
46 Will of Dorothy M. Macardle, 1375 P.R., Date of Grant 11 May 1959, National Archives of Ireland.

Two appreciations, by Frank Gallagher and Ann Keating, appeared in the *Irish Press*, as well as a tribute from Éamon de Valera. De Valera praised her heartfelt commitment to Irish independence, and her authorship of *The Irish Republic*. Frank Gallagher discussed her literary output and lauded her "great intelligence, deep loyalty, and profound integrity."[47] An unsigned obituary in the *Irish Press* also highlighted the importance of *The Irish Republic* and Dorothy's republican political activism.[48] Ann Keating's appreciation highlighted the personal attributes that made Dorothy a valued friend, such as her kindness and thoughtfulness.[49] Remembrances in the *Alexandra College Magazine* by former students also appeared, commenting on Dorothy's interest in literature and the supernatural, her charismatic personality, and her commitment to her students.[50]

References to Dorothy and her works occasionally appeared in the media and in articles and books in the years after her death. She was a character in the play *The History of Alexandra College*, performed in April 1966 to celebrate the centenary of the college. Philippa Gibbon, an Alexandra College student, portrayed Dorothy in a production that ran for four nights at the Royal Irish Academy of Music.[51] Phyllis Eason contributed a remembrance to the *Irish Times* in December 1968 to mark the tenth anniversary of Dorothy's death.[52] The writer Mary Manning, a former student, mentioned Dorothy in an article on Alexandra College in the *Irish Times* in 1978. Reminiscing on her student days in the early 1920s, she recalled Dorothy as an engaging teacher and made the famous claim that Dorothy was "hopelessly in love with de Valera."[53]

*The Irish Republic* was still considered relevant and politically useful by the government two decades after its initial publication. Éamon de Valera began lobbying for a reprint of *The Irish Republic*

47  "Dorothy Macardle, Writer, Worker For Freedom, Dies," *Irish Press*, 24 December 1958, 5.
48  "Dorothy Macardle, Writer, Worker For Freedom, Dies," *Irish Press*, 24 December 1958, 5.
49  "Funeral of Miss Dorothy Macardle," *Irish Press*, 25–27 December 1958, 7.
50  E.R.F., "Dorothy Macardle," *Alexandra College Dublin Magazine*, vol. 11 (June 1959); L.C. LeFanu, "Dorothy Macardle," *Alexandra College Dublin Magazine*, vol. 11 (December 1959).
51  Anne V. O'Connor and Susan M. Parkes, *Gladly Learn and Gladly Teach: Alexandra College and School, 1866–1966* (Dublin: Blackwater Press, 1984), 256–8.
52  *Irish Times*, 2 December 1968.
53  Mary Manning, "The Schoolgirls of Alexandra," *Irish Times*, 3 June 1978.

in early 1958, some months before Dorothy's death. Father Lawrence Flanagan, a Carmelite priest in the United States, had written to de Valera about the money subscribed to a trust fund under his control. De Valera thought the money could be used to subsidize a reprint of *The Irish Republic*. He noted that the lengthy book was costly to produce, and that the 1951 edition of the work, published by the *Irish Press*, would be out of print before too long. That would be unfortunate, de Valera wrote, "because it is the only really authoritative account of the period 1916–26."[54] He soon received a cheque for nearly two thousand dollars from Flanagan.[55] In 1965, the first American edition of *The Irish Republic* was published. Another Carmelite, Father Donald O'Callaghan, as well as the Ancient Order of Hibernians, offered to promote the new edition in the United States. The former Taoiseach explained to O'Callaghan why he thought it crucial to place the book in public libraries, universities, and newspaper offices throughout the United States. Journalists and documentary filmmakers researching modern Irish history for television, he wrote, tended to go to newspaper files from the time for information, but many newspapers in the United States during the Irish War of Independence were pro-British. This could be counteracted if *The Irish Republic* was widely available, as it gave "the truth of our struggle from an Irish point of view."[56]

*The Irish Republic* was also referenced by historians of contemporary Ireland in the years after Dorothy's death. The political implications of Irish history increasingly attracted the attention of historians during the crisis years in Northern Ireland, and her well-known republican history, which was reprinted in Britain in 1968,[57] was sometimes singled out for negative scrutiny. Historian Joe Lee assessed her as the "hagiographer royal to the Republic."[58] However, ten years later, historian Eunan O'Halpin contextualized *The Irish Republic* by noting that its political partisanship was no more egregious than works on contemporary Irish history written by non-

---

54 Éamon de Valera to Father Lawrence D. Flanagan, O. Carm., 20 March 1958. Cited in Alfred Isacsson, O. Carm., ed., *Irish Letters in the New York Carmelites' Archives* (Boca Raton, 1988), 13.

55 de Valera to Flanagan, 16 April 1958. Cited in Isacsson, 14.

56 de Valera to O'Callaghan, 4 May 1965. Cited in Isacsson, 48.

57 Dorothy Macardle, *The Irish Republic* (London: Corgi, 1968).

58 J.J. Lee, *Ireland, 1912–1985: Politics and Society* (Cambridge: Cambridge University Press, 1989), 270.

republican writers in the 1920s and 1930s. Dorothy Macardle, he wrote, was a highly competent researcher who was careful about documentation. Moreover, the book represented the constitutional republicanism of the Fianna Fáil government, not the dissident republicanism of those who refused to recognize the Irish Free State.[59] A new edition of *The Irish Republic* was published in 1999, with a foreword by Terry de Valera. Literary scholars as well as historians became more interested in Dorothy's work by the 1990s, in keeping with new scholarly interest in Irish women's writing, and her plays, stories, and novels began to receive critical attention.

Peter Berresford Ellis was the first writer to publish a biographical essay about Dorothy. He emphasized the significance of her novel *Uneasy Freehold*, and the film adaptation, *The Uninvited*, within literary history and the history of horror films.[60] Ellis had planned to write a biography of Dorothy in the 1980s, but found this was impossible, as Donald Macardle had destroyed his sister's personal papers.[61] However, the prospects for a biography became brighter in the 1990s when the National Library of Ireland acquired a great treasure, the diaries of Dorothy's friend Rosamond Jacob.

---

59 Eunan O'Halpin, "Historical Revisit: Dorothy Macardle, *The Irish Republic* (1937)," *Irish Historical Studies*, vol. 31, no. 123 (May 1999), 390.
60 Peter Tremayne [Peter Berresford Ellis], "A Reflection of Ghosts," in Stephen Jones and Jo Fletcher, eds., *Gaslight and Ghosts* (London: Robinson, 1988).
61 Ellis to author, 10 July 2000.

# Conclusion

DOROTHY MACARDLE WAS an important public intellectual in Ireland in the first half of the twentieth century. In addition to writing novels, plays, journalism and works of contemporary history, she was also a committed political and social activist, maintaining the stance of a critical insider within the Fianna Fáil party while simultaneously involving herself in struggles for women's rights, civil liberties, and intellectual freedom. As a journalist-historian with close ties to the political establishment, she played a key role in constructing and narrating the memory and meaning of the revolutionary period in Ireland during the middle decades of the twentieth century. She legitimized republican perspectives on recent Irish history in a book that gained iconic status and is itself a significant artifact of mid-twentieth century Ireland. Dorothy, through her book and journalism, reinforced notions of an Irish identity centered on a revolutionary and republican heritage.

Dorothy was an agent of social, cultural, and political change through her involvement in feminism and her advocacy of civil liberties and internationalism. Her internationalist humanitarianism reinforced a dimension of Irish identity that continued to grow throughout the twentieth century, and foreshadowed later Irish involvement in the United Nations and its humanitarian and peacekeeping missions, as well as independent Irish humanitarian groups with a global scope. Her life raises questions about older assumptions linking Irish nationalism with isolationism and insularity.

Dorothy's life shows many contradictions. She was a liberal feminist in Fianna Fáil, as well as an Irish republican with an English mother who strongly supported Britain and the Allies in World War II. She wrote republican and Fianna Fáil propaganda, and played a significant role in constructing positive images of de Valera and the Irish revolution, yet her fiction shows a more nuanced understanding of history and politics. While her stories and plays in the 1920s, for instance, raise questions about the glories of sacrifice in the service of nationalism, her political journalism shows she had not entirely rejected the ideal of sacrifice for the republic. Her fiction engaged Irish legends and mythology and interrogated mythical thinking, but she participated in the creation of an idealized image of Éamon de Valera, turning him into a mythical figure. Dorothy was raised in a late Victorian and Edwardian world, and in the twentieth century, she grappled with Victorian ideals, like many others of her generation. While she was a staunch democrat, for instance, she never entirely rejected the notions of social class she learned as a child raised in a wealthy family in the 1890s.

Dorothy's life was, in part, a journey involving a search for family and community and solidarity by someone who never quite fit in. She was not close to her own family in Dundalk, but found a new family in the community of intellectual women at Alexandra College in Dublin when she was a young woman. She drew closer to the community of Irish cultural nationalists and republicans, finding solidarity with them during the Irish War of Independence and Civil War, when she fell out with Alexandra College and became even more distant from her family. She separated herself from the community of dissident republicans when she joined Fianna Fáil. When she fell out with Fianna Fáil, she became more involved in the international humanitarian community. In her last years, she deepened her involvement in the community of progressive Irish intellectuals and political activists, and remained a critical supporter of Fianna Fáil and a humanitarian with an international outlook.

Dorothy's life was characterized by intellectual, creative, and humanitarian achievement, as well as tensions between political and social realities and ideals that manifested themselves in her work. Donald Macardle may have destroyed Dorothy's papers, but her voice lives on. What happened to her toy theatre is anyone's guess, but with all the real drama in her life, the fate of the Victorian toy theatre hardly matters.

# Select Bibliography

## PRIMARY SOURCES

### MANUSCRIPT

**Ireland**
*Alexandra College Dublin*
Dorothy Macardle file

*General Register Office, Dublin*
Birth certificate of Dorothy Macardle
Marriage certificate of Thomas Macardle and Minnie Lucy Ross

*National Archives of Ireland*
Census of Ireland, 1901, Louth
Census of Ireland, 1911, Louth
Will of Thomas Macardle
Will of Dorothy Macardle
Dorothy Macardle, Bureau of Military History Witness Statement
Department of An Taoiseach Papers

*National Library of Ireland*
Frank Gallagher Papers
Rosamond Jacob Papers
Sheehy Skeffington Papers

*RTÉ Written Archives*
Broadcast talks by Dorothy Macardle

*Trinity College Dublin, Manuscripts Department*
Childers Papers

*University College Dublin Archives*
Máire Comerford Papers
Lily O'Brennan Papers
Kathleen O'Connell Papers
Terence MacSwiney Papers
Moss Twomey Papers

**England**
*BBC Written Archives Centre*
Dorothy Macardle file

*General Register Office, Southport*
Marriage certificate of James Clarke Hicks and Isabella Lucy Ross
Birth certificate of Minnie Lucy Hicks
Death certificate of Minnie Lucy Macardle

*National Archives, Kew*
Census of England, 1881
Census of Scotland, 1891
War Office 339/28290

*John Rylands Library, Manchester*
Correspondence of Dorothy Macardle with the editor of the
*Manchester Guardian*

*Tameside Archive*
MR 1/3/2/6
MR 3/26/168

**United States**
*Columbia University, New York*
Carnegie Endowment for International Peace Papers

*Mills College Archive, Oakland, California*
Dorothy Macardle, Mills College Commencement Address

PRINTED
**Newspapers/Journals**
*Alexandra College Dublin Magazine*
*Dublin Magazine*
*Dundalk Democrat*
*Éire*
*Irish Independent*
*Irish Press*
*Irish Times*
*Nation*
*New Statesman and Nation*
*New York Times*
*An Phoblacht*
*Sinn Féin*
*Times*

**Works by Dorothy Macardle**

*Earth-bound: Nine Stories of Ireland.* Worcester, Mass.: Harrigan Press, 1924.

*Tragedies of Kerry.* 1924: Dublin, Irish Freedom Press, 1988.

*The Irish Republic.* London: Victor Gollancz, 1937.

*Uneasy Freehold.* London: Peter Davies, 1941.

*The Seed Was Kind.* London: Peter Davies, 1944.

*Fantastic Summer.* London: Peter Davies, 1946.

*Children of Europe.* Boston: Beacon Press, 1951.

*Dark Enchantment.* Garden City, New York: Doubleday & Company, 1953.

"The Crystal Star." *Illustrated London News*, vol. 229, 9 November 1956.

"James Connolly and Patrick Pearse." In Conor Cruise O'Brien, ed., *The Shaping of Modern Ireland.* London: Routledge and Kegan Paul, 1960.

*Shakespeare, Man and Boy.* London: Faber, 1960.

## SECONDARY SOURCES

Ankarloo, Bengt, and Stuart Clark, eds. *Witchcraft and Magic in Europe in the Twentieth Century.* Philadelphia: University of Pennsylvania Press, 1999.

Backus, Margot Gayle. *The Gothic Family Romance: Heterosexuality, Child Sacrifice, and the Anglo-Irish Colonial Order*. Durham: Duke University Press, 1999.

Beaumont, Catriona. "Women and the Politics of Equality: The Irish Women's Movement, 1930–1943." In Maryann Gialanella Valiulis and Mary O'Dowd, eds. *Women in Irish History: Essays in Honour of Margaret MacCurtain*. Dublin: Wolfhound Press, 1997. 173–88.

Berenbaum, Michael. *A Mosaic of Victims*. New York: New York University Press, 1990.

Berg, Maxine. *A Woman in History: Eileen Power, 1889–1940*. Cambridge: Cambridge University Press, 1996.

Bhreatnach, Aoife. *Becoming Conspicuous: Irish Travellers, Society, and the State*. Dublin: University College Dublin Press, 2006.

Black, Maggie. *Children First: The Story of UNICEF, Past and Present*. Oxford: Oxford University Press, 1996.

Bourke, Angela. *Maeve Brennan: Homesick at the New Yorker*. London: Jonathan Cape, 2004.

Bowen, Elizabeth. *Seven Winters and Afterthoughts*. New York: Alfred A. Knopf, 1962.

Brennan, Robert. *Allegiance*. Dublin: Browne and Nolan, 1950.

Clear, Caitríona. *Women of the House*. Dublin: Irish Academic Press, 2000.

Cobb, Richard. *A Classical Education*. London: Chatto and Windus, 1985.

Coogan, Tim Pat. *De Valera: Long Fellow, Long Shadow*. London, 1995.

Cronin, Seán. *Frank Ryan: The Search for the Republic*. Dublin, 1980.

Davies, Owen. *Witchcraft, Magic, and Culture, 1736–1951*. Manchester: Manchester University Press, 1999.

Deale, Kenneth. *Memorable Irish Trials*. London: Constable, 1960.

Diamond, Hanna. *Women and the Second World War in France*. New York: Pearson, 1999.

Doyle, Damian. "Rosamond Jacob (1888–1960)." In Mary Cullen and Maria Luddy, eds., *Female Activists: Irish Women and Change, 1900–1960*. Dublin: The Woodfield Press, 2001. 169–79.

Dyhouse, Carol. *Girls Growing Up in Late Victorian and Edwardian England*. London: Routledge and Kegan Paul, 1981.

——. *Feminism and the Family in England, 1880–1939*. Oxford: Basil Blackwell, 1989.

——. *No Distinction of Sex? Women in British Universities, 1870–1939*. London: UCL Press, 1995.

Fagan, Kieran. "Unnatural Born Killers." *Irish Times*, 13 December 1994, 13.

Fallon, Charlotte. "Civil War Hungerstrikes: Women and Men." *Éire-Ireland*, vol. 22 (1987).

Feeney, William. *Drama in Hardwicke Street: A History of the Irish Theatre Company*. London and Toronto: Associated University Presses, 1984.

Fitzpatrick, David, ed. *Ireland and the First World War*. Dublin, 1986.

Foster, R.F. *Paddy and Mr. Punch: Connections in English and Irish History*. New York: Penguin, 1993.

Glendinning, Victoria. *Elizabeth Bowen: Portrait of a Writer*. London: Phoenix, 1977.

Gregory, Adrian, and Senia Paseta, eds. *Ireland and the Great War: 'A War to Unite Us All'?* Manchester: Manchester University Press, 2002.

Grubgeld, Elizabeth. *Anglo-Irish Autobiography: Class, Gender, and the Forms of Narrative*. Syracuse: Syracuse University Press, 2004.

Hall, Donal. *World War I and Nationalist Politics in County Louth, 1914–1920*. Dublin: Four Courts Press, 2005.

Hanley, Brian. *The IRA, 1926–1936*. Dublin: Four Courts Press, 2002.

Hayes, Alan, ed. *The Years Flew By: The Recollections of Madame Sidney Gifford Czira*. Galway: Arlen House, 2000.

Hazelgrove, Jenny. *Spiritualism and British Society Between the Wars*. Manchester: Manchester University Press, 2000.

Hogan, Robert, and Richard Burnham. *The Art of the Amateur: 1916–1920*. Dublin: Dolmen Press, 1984.

——. *The Years of O'Casey: 1921–1926*. Dublin: Dolmen Press, 1992.

Hopkinson, Michael. *The Irish War of Independence*. Dublin: Gill and Macmillan, 2002.

——. *Green Against Green: The Irish Civil War*. Dublin: Gill and Macmillan, 1988.

Hoppen, K. Theodore. *Ireland Since 1800: Conflict and Conformity*. London and New York: Longman, 1989.

Horner, Avril, and Sue Zlosnik. *Daphne du Maurier: Writing, Identity, and the Gothic Imagination*. New York: St. Martin's Press, 1998.

Kavka, Misha. "The Gothic on Screen." In Jerrold E. Hogle, ed., *The Cambridge Companion to Gothic Fiction*. New York: Cambridge University Press, 2002.

Kelly, Adrian. *Compulsory Irish: Language and Education in Ireland, 1870s–1970s*. Dublin: Irish Academic Press, 2002.

Keogh, Dermot, Finbarr O'Shea, and Carmel Quinlan, eds. *The Lost Decade: Ireland in the 1950s*. Cork: Mercier Press, 2004.

Kurth, Peter. *American Cassandra: The Life of Dorothy Thompson*. Boston: Little, Brown, and Company, 1990.

Lagrou, Pieter. *The Legacy of Nazi Occupation: Patriotic Memory and National Recovery in Western Europe, 1945–1965*. Cambridge: Cambridge University Press, 2000.

Lee, J.J. *Ireland, 1912–1985: Politics and Society*. Cambridge: Cambridge University Press, 1989.

Leeney, Cathy. "Violence on the Abbey Theatre Stage: The National Project and the Critic; Two Case Studies." *Modern Drama* 47:4, Winter 2004. 587.

Levitas, Ben. *The Theatre of Nation: Irish Drama and Cultural Nationalism, 1890–1916*. Oxford: Clarendon Press, 2002.

Malone, A.E. *The Irish Drama*. New York: Charles Scribner's Sons, 1929.

Manning, Mary. *Mount Venus*. Boston: Houghton Mifflin, 1938.

——. "The Schoolgirls of Alexandra." *Irish Times*, 3 June 1978.

Marten, James, ed. *Children and War: A Historical Anthology*. New York: New York University Press, 2002.

Mathews, P.J. *Revival: The Abbey Theatre, Sinn Féin, the Gaelic League, and the Co-operative Movement*. Cork: Cork University Press, 2003.

Maume, Patrick. *The Long Gestation: Irish Nationalist Life, 1891–1918*. New York: St. Martin's Press, 1999.

McCoole, Sinéad. *No Ordinary Women: Irish Female Activists in the Revolutionary Years, 1900–1923*. Madison: University of Wisconsin Press, 2003.

McGarry, Fearghal. *Frank Ryan*. Dundalk: Dundalgan Press, 2002.

Meaney, Geraldine. "The Sons of Cuchulainn: Violence, the Family, and the Irish Canon." *Éire-Ireland* 41:1&2, Spring/Summer 2006.

Miller, Carole. "'Geneva: the Key to Equality': Interwar Feminists and the League of Nations." *Women's History Review*, vol. 3, no. 2, 1994. 219–45.

Mitchell, Sally. *The New Girl: Girls' Culture in England, 1880–1915*. New York: Columbia University Press, 1995.

Molidor, Jennifer. "Violence, Silence, and Sacrifice: the Mother-Daughter Relationship in the Short Fiction of Modern Irish Women Writers, 1890–1980." PhD Dissertation, University of Notre Dame, 2007.

——. "Dying for Ireland: Violence, Silence, and Female Solidarity in the Stories of Dorothy Macardle." *New Hibernia Review*, forthcoming.

Molohan, Cathy. *Germany and Ireland, 1945–1955: Two Nations' Friendship*. Dublin: Irish Academic Press, 1999.

Mulvihill, Margaret. *Charlotte Despard: a Biography*. London: Pandora Press, 1989.

Murray, Patrick. "Obsessive Historian: Éamon de Valera and the Policing of His Reputation." *Proceedings of the Royal Irish Academy*, vol. 101C, 37–65, 2001.

Nicholas, Sian. *The Echo of War: Homefront Propaganda and the Wartime BBC, 1939–1945*. Manchester: Manchester University Press, 1996.

Novick, Peter. *The Holocaust in American Life*. Boston: Houghton Mifflin, 2000.

O'Brien, Mark. *De Valera, Fianna Fáil, and the Irish Press*. Dublin: Irish Academic Press, 2001.

Ó Broin, Léon. *Protestant Revolutionaries in Ireland: the Stopford Connection*. Dublin: Gill and Macmillan, 1985.

O'Connor, Anne V., and Susan M. Parkes. *Gladly Learn and Gladly Teach: Alexandra College and School, 1866–1966*. Dublin: Blackwater Press, 1984.

Ó Duigneáin, Proinnsios. *Linda Kearns: A Revolutionary Irish Woman*. Nure, Co. Leitrim: Drumlin Publications, 2002.

O'Halpin, Eunan. "Historical Revisit: Dorothy Macardle, *The Irish Republic* (1937)." *Irish Historical Studies*, vol. 31, no. 123, May 1999.

Ó hÓgartaigh, Margaret. *Kathleen Lynn: Irishwoman, Patriot, Doctor.* Dublin: Irish Academic Press, 2006.

Owens, Rosemary Cullen. *Smashing Times: a History of the Irish Women's Suffrage Movement, 1889–1922.* Dublin: Attic Press, 1984.

Richardson, Joanna. *Enid Starkie.* New York: Macmillan, 1973.

Rupp, Leila. *Worlds of Women: the Making of an International Women's Movement.* Princeton: Princeton University Press, 1997.

Sheehan, Aideen. "Cumann na mBan, Policies and Activities." In David Fitzpatrick, ed., *Revolution? Ireland 1917–1923.* Dublin: Leinster Leader Ltd, 1990.

Smith, Bonnie G. *The Gender of History: Men, Women, and Historical Practice.* Cambridge, Mass.: Harvard University Press, 1998.

Smith, James M. "The Politics of Sexual Knowledge: the Origins of Ireland's Containment Culture and the Carrigan Report (1931)." *Journal of the History Of Sexuality*, vol. 13, no. 2 (April 2004).

Smith, Nadia Clare. *A 'Manly Study'? Irish Women Historians, 1868–1949.* Basingstoke and New York: Palgrave Macmillan, 2006.

Stableford, Brian. "Dorothy Macardle." In David Pringle, ed., *St. James Guide to Horror, Ghost, and Gothic Writers.* Detroit: St. James Press, 1998. 382.

Starkie, Enid. *A Lady's Child.* London: Faber and Faber, 1941.

Swift, Carolyn. *Stage by Stage.* Dublin, 1985.

Travers, Pauric. *Éamon de Valera.* Dundalk: Dundalgan Press, 1994.

Tremayne, Peter. "A Reflection of Ghosts." In Stephen Jones and Jo Fletcher, eds. *Gaslight and Ghosts.* London: Robinson, 1988.

Walsh, Éibhear, *Kate O'Brien, A Writing Life* (Dublin: Irish Academic Press, 2006) 109.

Walsh, Oonagh. "Testimony From Imprisoned Women." In David Fitzpatrick, ed., *Revolution? Ireland 1917–1923.* Dublin: Leinster Leader Ltd, 1990.

Ward, Margaret. *Unmanageable Revolutionaries: Women and Irish Nationalism.* London: Pluto Press, 1983.

——. *Maud Gonne: Ireland's Joan of Arc.* London: Pandora Press, 1990.

Welch, Robert. *The Abbey Theatre, 1899–1999: Form and Pressure.* Oxford: Oxford University Press, 1999.

Weindling, Paul, ed. *International Health Organizations and Movements, 1918–1939.* Cambridge: Cambridge University Press, 1995.

Wills, Clair. "Women Writers and the Death of Rural Ireland: Realism and Nostalgia in the 1940s." *Éire-Ireland* 41: 1&2, Spring/Summer 2006.

Winter, Jay M. *Sites of Memory, Sites of Mourning: The Great War in European Cultural History.* Cambridge: Cambridge University Press, 1995.

Wyman, Mark. *DPs: Europe's Displaced Persons, 1945–1951.* Ithaca: Cornell University Press, 1998.

# Index